Instructor's Manual with Test Bank to Accompany

INTRODUCTORY ALGEBRA

Derek I. Bloomfield
Orange County Community College

Prepared by
Maria Blon
Orange County Community College

West Publishing Company
Minneapolis/St. Paul   New York   Los Angeles   San Francisco

D1402532

WEST'S COMMITMENT TO THE ENVIRONMENT

In 1906, West Publishing Company began recycling materials left over from the production of books. This began a tradition of efficient and responsible use of resources. Today, up to 95% of our legal books and 70% of our college and school texts are printed on recycled, acid-free stock. West also recycles nearly 22 million pounds of scrap paper annually—the equivalent of 181,717 trees. Since the 1960s, West has devised ways to capture and recycle waste inks, solvents, oils, and vapors created in the printing process. We also recycle plastics of all kinds, wood, glass, corrugated cardboard, and batteries, and have eliminated the use of Styrofoam book packaging. We at West are proud of the longevity and the scope of commitment to the environment.

Production, Prepress, Printing and Binding by West Publishing Company.

 PRINTED ON 10% POST CONSUMER RECYCLED PAPER

Acknowledgements

I would like to thank Derek for asking me to do this project. I would also like to thank my husband, Tom for his support and help with proofreading. Lastly, I thank my daughter Carina for being such a good baby and allowing me to finish this project.

Table of Contents

Chapter Topics, Review Sheets, Chapter Tests, Answers

Test Bank: Multiple Choice, Problems, Answers

Using this Instructor's Manual

For each chapter of Bloomfield's *Introductory Algebra* text, this Instructor's Manual includes a list of section topics, a review sheet, a chapter test, and a test bank with both multiple choice and completion problems.

Each multiple choice question has the answer and section that the problem came from labeled to the right of the questions. The answers were placed on the right hand side so that if you choose to photo copy these problems, you can easily cover the answers with a piece of paper.

The test bank questions are also available on a computer disk, if you choose to prepare tests on the computer instead of photo copying the pages of this book.

Homework Assignments

Each section of Introductory Algebra is followed by a set of exercises corresponding to the section. I suggest that students work the odd numbered problems for homework, since they can check these answers in the back of the book. Some sections of the text include "Mental Mathematics" exercises. These exercises can be used by the instructor during class to give each student a chance to participate by doing a problem.

At the end of each chapter, Bloomfield has included a set of review exercises which are keyed to each section, plus an achievement test. I suggest that students do the achievement test for homework, and work the review exercises for the sections that they need extra practice.

Chapter 1 Topics

Chapter 1 Review Sheet

Draw a number line and locate the following points:
1. 3.5   2. 0   3. -1

Represent each quantity with a signed number:

4. The climber scaled a 300 foot cliff.   4._____

5. You lose forty dollars at a slot machine in Las Vegas.   5._____

Find the absolute value of each of the following:

6. 14.6   6._____

7. -23   7._____

8. 0   8._____

Insert < or > between each pair of numbers to make a true statement.

9. -22   15   9._____

10. 5   0   10._____

11. -7   -9   11._____

Evaluate each of the following:

12. -3 - 15   12._____

13. (-33)(2)   13._____

14. 13 + (-3)   14._____

15. (-27) ÷ (-3)   15._____

16. -18 - (-216)   16._____

17. (0)(-50)   17._____

18. (25) ÷ 0   18._____

19. $-2\frac{1}{2} + \frac{3}{4}$

19._____

20. $-\frac{2}{3} \div -\frac{4}{7}$

20._____

21. $-22 + 3 - 11 - (-5) + 30$

21._____

22. $(5)(1)(-2)(-1)(4)$

22._____

23. $2.9 - 13.87$

23._____

24. $(-4)^2$

24._____

25. -3^3

25._____

26. $-\sqrt{36}$

26._____

27. $\sqrt[3]{-8}$

27._____

28. $10 - 6.5$

28._____

29. $4(-3) - (-2)^2 + 15 \div (4-7)$

29._____

30. $28 \div 7(-4) + 14 - (-2)$

30._____

31. $12(-2) + 5\{1-3(-5) + 2(3-4)\}$

31._____

32. Bronwyn opens her first checking account with two
hundred dollars. Her bank charges a monthly fee of $5,
she writes a check for $53.76, and deposits $34.20.
What is her balance at the end of the first month?

32._____

33. A Quantas airplane flies at an altitude of 1500 feet. During
rough weather, the plane dropped 300 feet, rose 150 feet,
rose another 200 feet and finally dropped 120 feet. What is
the final altitude of the airplane?

33._____

34. Latasha buys a stereo on a payment plan. Each month, she
pays $35. If the stereo will be paid for in a year and a half,
how much will she have paid for her stereo?

34._____

Chapter 1 Test

Draw a number line and locate the following points:
1. 4   2. -5   3. 0

Represent each quantity with a signed number:
4. The diver swam 25 feet below sea level.   4._____

5. You win four hundred dollars in the lottery.   5._____

Find the absolute value of each of the following:
6. -12   6._____

7. 0   7._____

8. 3.9   8._____

Insert < or > between each pair of numbers to make a true statement.
9. 3   -4   9._____

10. -15   -5   10._____

11. 0   -1   11._____

Evaluate each of the following:
12. 5 - 11   12._____

13. (-21)(-2)   13._____

14. -4 - (-3)   14._____

15. (25) ÷ (-5)   15._____

16. -14 - 12   16._____

17. (-27)(0)   17._____

18. (-14) ÷ 0   18._____

19. $-\sqrt[3]{27}$

20. $\sqrt{100}$

19._____

20._____

21. $14 - 3 + 7 + (-11) - 5$

21._____

22. $(2)(-1)(-3)(1)(-4)$

22._____

23. $14.73 - 21.9$

23._____

24. $(-3)^3$

24._____

25. -2^4

25._____

26. $-\dfrac{5}{6} \div \dfrac{25}{54}$

26._____

27. $\dfrac{2}{3} - 1\dfrac{3}{4}$

27._____

28. $4 - 2.6$

28._____

29. $10 + 3^2 - 4(2)$

29._____

30. $10 - 15 \div 5(3)$

30._____

31. $4 - 2[\, 7 - (10 + 2)\,]$

31._____

32. Nikia is overdrawn by \$12.16 in her checking account. The bank charges her \$10 for being overdrawn. If she deposits \$25 in her account, what will be her new balance?

32._____

33. Mark buys a car. Each month, he pays \$250 towards his car. How much will he have paid on his car after 1 year?

33._____

34. The Sun-Ye stock increases 3/4 point, falls 1/2 point, increases 1.5 points and finally falls 1/4 point. What is the net change in the stock price?

34._____

6

Answers

Chapter 1 Review Sheet

1, 2, & 3

4. +300 feet   5. -$40   6. 14.6   7. 23   8. 0   9. <   10. >   11. >   12. -18   13. -66

14. 10   15. 9   16. 198   17. 0   18. undefined   19. -1 3/4   20. 7/6   21. 5   22. 40

23. -10.97   24. 16   25. -27   26. -6   27. -2   28. 3.5   29. -21   30. 0   31. 46

32. $175.44   33. 1430 feet   34. $630

Chapter 1 Test

1, 2, & 3

4. -25 feet   5. +$400   6. 12   7. 0   8. 3.9   9. >   10. <   11. >   12. -6   13. 42

14. -1   15. -5   16. -26   17. 0   18. undefined   19. -3   20. 10   21. 2   22. -24

23. -7.17   24. -27   25. -16   26. -9/5   27. -1 1/12   28. 1.4   29. 11   30. 1   31. 14

32. $2.84   33. $3000   34. 1.5 points

7

Chapter 2 Topics

Chapter 2 Review Sheet

Evaluate:

1. $V = \frac{4}{3}\pi r^2 h$ if $\pi = 3.14$, $r = 10$, $h = 3$

1._____

2. $Z = 3T - 6K$ if $T = 7$, $K = 3$

2._____

Evaluate when $a = -3$, $b = -1$, $c = 5$
3. $4a - 9b - 2c$

3._____

4. $-2b^3 + 3a^2c - ac$

4._____

Combine like terms:
5. $7a^3b - 3ab^2 + 9a^2b + 4a^3b$

5._____

6. $4w - 5r + 11 - 7r - 8w - 15$

6._____

7. $12ab - (-15b) + 3a + 4b - 7ab$

7._____

Simplify where possible:
8. a^2b^9

8._____

9. $x^5x^6w^3$

9._____

10. $a^5b^2a^8$

10._____

11. x^2wxy

11._____

12. $(-3ab^5)(5a^3b^4)$

12._____

13. $-2wy(-7w + 4y^6)$

13._____

14. $(x)(15xy^3)(-2y^2)$

14._____

15. $(-7x^2)(5x^2 - 3x - 7)$

15._____

16. $(-4a^3 + 11ab - 12)(3a^3b)$

16._____

17. $-(-3x^4 - 11x^2 - 5x + 20)$

17._____

Simplify:
18. $8 - 4(3x - 5) + 16x$

18._____

19. $x(-2x + y) - 6(4x^2 - 5y)$

19._____

20. -4[5x - 4(x - 3)]

21. - { 1 - 7[-x + 4(3x - 2)] } - 4x

22. The temperature in Sydney, Australia on March 5th
was 40°C. What is the equivalent Fahrenheit temperature,
using $F = \frac{9}{5}C + 32$?

20._____

21._____

22._____

Chapter 2 Test

Evaluate:

1. $S = \frac{1}{2}gt^2$ if $g = 32$, $t = 2$

1._____

2. $P = 2L + 2w$ if $L = 7$, $W = 7$

2._____

Evaluate when $a = 4$, $b = -2$, $c = -5$

3. $2a - 3b + 7c$

3._____

4. $-3b^2 - 2a^2b + 4ac$

4._____

Combine like terms:

5. $5a^2b - 3ab^2 - 11a^2b + 4ab$

5._____

6. $6x - 3y + 4 - 11y + 6x - 4$

6._____

7. $7wx - 5 + 4wx - (-10w) + 11$

7._____

Simplify where possible:

8. a^2a^5

8._____

9. $w^4w^6w^9$

9._____

10. $a^2b^2c^3$

10._____

11. x^ax^b

11._____

12. $(-2ab^3)(-5a^2b^4)$

12._____

13. $2wy(-3w + 5y^3)$

13._____

14. $(x^2)(-4xy^3)(-y^2)$

14._____

15. $(-3x^3)(5x^2 - 3x - 7)$

15._____

16. $(-4a^3 + 11ab - 12)(-2a^2b)$

16._____

17. $- (10x^4 - 11x^2 + 5x - 20)$

17._____

Simplify:

18. $3 - 2(x - 5) + 11x$

18._____

19. $x(2x - y) - 3(-2x^2 + 5y)$

19._____

11

20. -2[3x - 4(x + 5)]   20._____

21. - { 3 - 5[2x + 4(x - 2)] } + 4x   21._____

22. The temperature in Middletown, New York on March 5th
    was 41°F. What is the equivalent Celsius temperature,   22._____
    using $C = \frac{5}{9}(F - 32)$?

Answers

Chapter 2 Review Sheet

1. 1256   2. 3   3. -13   4. 152   5. $11a^3 - 3ab^2 + 9a^2b$ 6. -4w -12r -4   7. 5ab + 19b +3a

8. can't simplify   9. $x^{11}w^3$ 10. $a^{13}b^2$ 11. x^{2w+y} 12. $-15a^4b^9$ 13. $14w^2y - 8wy^7$

14. $-30x^2y^5$ 15. $-35x^4 + 21x^3 + 49x^2$ 16. $-12a^6b + 33a^4b^2 - 36a^3b$

17. $3x^4 + 11x^2 + 5x - 20$ 18. 4x + 28   19. $-26x^2 + xy + 30y$ 20. -4x - 48   21. -57 + 73x

22. 104ºF

Chapter 2 Test

1. 64   2. 28   3. -21   4. -28   5. $-6a^2b - 3ab^2 + 4ab$ 6. 12x - 14y   7. 11wx + 6 + 10w

8. a^7 9. w^{19} 10. can't simplify   11. x^{a+b} 12. $10a^3b^7$ 13. $-6w^2y + 10wy^4$ 14. $4x^3y^5$

15. $-15x^5 + 9x^4 + 21x^3$ 16. $8a^5b - 22a^3b^2 + 24a^2b$ 17. $-10x^4 + 11x^2 - 5x + 20$

18. 9x + 13   19. $8x^2 -xy -15y$ 20. 2x + 40   21. 34x - 43   22. 5º C

Chapter 3 Topics

Chapter 3 Review Sheet

Determine if x = -2 is a solution to:
1. $x - 13 = -3 - 4x$

1._____

2. $5x + 2 = 2(x - 2)$

2._____

Solve each equation:
3. $x - 3 = -9$

3._____

4. $\dfrac{3y}{-5} = -12$

4._____

5. $4x - 5 = -2 + 7x$

5._____

6. $4 - 10x = 24$

6._____

7. $4(3x + 1) = -2(5 - x)$

7._____

8. $\dfrac{3}{5}x - 2 = \dfrac{1}{3} - \dfrac{7}{10}x$

8._____

9. $0.4y - 1.25 = 0.9 - 5y$

9._____

10. $-\dfrac{2}{3}(3x + 1) = \dfrac{1}{4}(9 - 2x) + 1$

10._____

Classify the following as conditional, an identity, or as a contradiction. Solve the conditional equations.
11. $6x - 10 = 4 - 5(x - 3)$

11._____

12. $5(x - 3) - x = 4x + 7$

12._____

13. $15 + 7x = -3x + 5(3 + 2x)$

13._____

Solve:
14. $5t - 4st = 11r$ for s

14._____

15. $V = \dfrac{4}{3}\pi r^3$ for π

15._____

16. $4x - 5 < 6(5 - x)$

16._____

17. $\dfrac{1}{6}x - \dfrac{2}{3} \geq 5 + \dfrac{2}{5}x$

17._____

Chapter 3 Test

Determine if x = -3 is a solution to:

1. $4(x + 1) = 5 - 3x$

2. $2x + 11 = 2 - x$

Solve each equation:

3. $x + 7 = -4$

4. $\dfrac{y}{-4} = 6$

5. $5x + 3 = 7x - 5$

6. $3 - 6x = -9$

7. $-3(x + 7) = 5(4 - 3x)$

8. $\dfrac{1}{2}x + 4 = \dfrac{2}{3} - \dfrac{1}{4}x$

9. $0.1y - 0.9 = 0.3 + 0.2y$

10. $\dfrac{1}{3}(x + 2) = -\dfrac{1}{2}(3 - 2x)$

Classify the following as conditional, an identity, or as a contradiction. Solve the conditional equations.

11. $5 - 2(2x + 7) = -4x + 3$

12. $3(x - 4) + 5x = 6x + 7$

13. $-4 + 5x = -3x + 4(1 + 2x)$

Solve:

14. $3a - 4b = 7c$ for b

15. $A = \dfrac{1}{2}bh$ for b

16. $2x - 3 \geq 5x + 9$

17. $\dfrac{2}{3}x - \dfrac{1}{2} < 3 - \dfrac{1}{2}x$

1._____

2._____

3._____

4._____

5._____

6._____

7._____

8._____

9._____

10._____

11._____

12._____

13._____

14._____

15._____

16._____

17._____

Answers

Chapter 3 Review Sheet

1. no   2. yes   3. -6   4. 20   5. -1   6. -2   7. -1.4   8. 70/39   9. 43/108   10. -2

11. conditional, x = 29/11   12. contradiction   13. identity   14. $(11r - 5t) / (-4t)$

15. $3V / (4r^3)$ 16. x < 3.5   17. x ≤ -170 / 7

Chapter 3 Test

1. no   2. yes   3. -11   4. -24   5. 4   6. 2   7. 41/12   8. -40/9   9. -12   10. 13/4

11. contradiction   12. conditional, x = 19/2   13. contradiction   14. $(7c - 3a) / (-4)$ 15. $2A / h$

16. x ≤ -4   17. x < 3

Chapter 4 Topics

Chapter 4 Review Sheet

Write each English sentence as a mathematical equation.

1. Five less than three times a number is fourteen.

1._____

2. When the sum of twelve and a number is multiplied by three, the result is the number less two.

2._____

Solve each of the following:

3. Twice a number, less three is the same as the number divided by two. Find the number.

3._____

4. Find three consecutive odd integers whose sum is -63.

4._____

5. If you earn grades of: 86, 95, and 77 on your first three exams, what must you earn on the fourth to average 85 on the four exams?

5._____

6. 45% of what number is 31.05?

6._____

7. What percent of 450 is 103.5?

7._____

8. A tractor sells for $56,000. If the tax rate is 4.5%, how much will the tax be on the tractor?

8._____

9. What is the ratio of 400 centimeters to 5 meters?

9._____

10. Solve: $\dfrac{w}{7} = \dfrac{30}{21}$

10._____

11. Mary Jo can bike 12 miles in 25 minutes. How long would it take her to bike a century (100 miles) at this same rate?

11._____

12. An evergreen tree grows 3.5 inches every two years. How much would the tree grow in 16 years at this rate?

12._____

13. Convert 5 yards to inches.

13._____

14. Change 60 miles per hour to feet per second.

14._____

15. How many cubic inches are in 3 gallons?

15._____

16. How many square yards of carpet are needed to cover a room which is 40 feet by 70 feet?

16._____

Chapter 4 Test

Write each English sentence as a mathematical equation.
1. Seven more than twice a number is twelve.

1._____

2. When the quantity of a number less one is divided by two, the result is the same as the product of the number and forty.

2._____

Solve each of the following:
3. Twenty three is the same as three less than twice a number. Find the number.

3._____

4. Find two consecutive odd integers whose sum is 188.

4._____

5. If you earn grades of: 91, 70, and 82 on your first three exams, what must you earn on the fourth to average 80 on the four exams?

5._____

6. 30% of 65 is what number?

6._____

7. What percent of 120 is 43.2?

7._____

8. The price for an Omega TV is $340. The sales tax is 5%. How much will the tax be on the TV?

8._____

9. What is the ratio of 2 yards to 10 inches?

9._____

10. Solve: $\dfrac{3}{x} = \dfrac{15}{20}$

10._____

11. On a trip, a family drove 441 kilometers in 7 hours. How many kilometers per hour did they average for their trip?

11._____

12. A drug that is given according to body weight is given at a rate of 3 milligrams per 40 pounds. How much of the drug should be given to a 120 pound woman?

12._____

13. Convert 27 inches to yards.

13._____

14. Change 85 feet per second to miles per hour.

14._____

15. How many cubic centimeters are in 6 cubic meters?

15._____

16. How many square feet of linoleum are needed to cover a room which is 10 feet by 12 feet?

16._____

Answers

Chapter 4 Review Sheet

1. $3x - 5 = 14$ 2. $3(12 + x) = x - 2$ 3. 2   4. -23, -21, -19   5. 82   6. 69   7. 23%

8. $2520   9. 4/5   10. 10   11. 208 1/3 minutes or 3 hours and 28 1/3 minutes   12. 28 in.

13. 180 inches   14. 88 feet per second   15. 693.05 cubic inches   16. 311.11 square yards

Chapter 4 Test

1. $2x + 7 = 12$ 2. $(x - 1) \div 2 = 40x$ 3. 13   4. 93, 95   5. 77   6. 19.5   7. 36%   8. $17

9. 36/5   10. 4   11. 63 km per hour   12. 9 milligrams   13. 0.75 yards   14. 57.95 mph

15. 6,000,000 cubic centimeters   16. 120 square feet

Chapter 5 Topics

Chapter 5 Review Sheet

Simplify, leaving answers with only positive exponents.

1. $x^{-7}x^3$

1._____

2. $(-3xy^3)^2$

2._____

3. $(2a^5b^{-3})^2$

3._____

4. $\dfrac{b^5}{b^{11}}$

4._____

5. x^8x

5._____

6. $4y^{-6}$

6._____

7. $\left(\dfrac{2w}{z}\right)^{-4}$

7._____

8. $\left(\dfrac{25f^{-8}g^{10}}{-35f^{-6}g^3}\right)^0$

8._____

9. $\dfrac{12x^3y^0}{-4x^{-3}}$

9._____

10. $\dfrac{2}{z^{-5}}$

10._____

11. $\left(\dfrac{-2}{5}\right)^{-3}$

11._____

12. $\left(\dfrac{6c^{-5}}{4c^{-3}}\right)^{-3}$

12._____

Write in Scientific Notation:

13. 657,000,000,000

13._____

14. 0.0013

14._____

Write in ordinary notation:

15. 5.37×10^{-4}

15._____

16. 8.95×10^{7}

16._____

Calculate using scientific notation and rules of exponents.
Write your answer in scientific notation.

17. (21,000,000,000)(0.0003)

17._____

18. $\dfrac{(0.000006)(2,200,000,000)}{(0.000033)}$

18._____

Chapter 5 Test

Simplify, leaving answers with only positive exponents.

1. $x^5 x^{-3}$

2. $(3x^5 y)^3$

3. $(-7a^{-5} b^9)^2$

4. $\dfrac{b^9}{b^3}$

5. $x^5 x$

6. $-8y^{-4}$

7. $\left(\dfrac{a}{b}\right)^{-1}$

8. $\left(\dfrac{5a^{-2}b}{a^{-6}}\right)^2$

9. $\dfrac{-9x^2}{3x^0}$

10. $\left(\dfrac{4}{8}\right)^{-4}$

11. $\dfrac{16}{c^{-5}}$

12. $\left(\dfrac{56c^{-5}}{9a^3 c^{-3}}\right)^0$

1._____

2._____

3._____

4._____

5._____

6._____

7._____

8._____

9._____

10._____

11._____

12._____

Write in Scientific Notation:

13. 0.000058

13._____

14. 236,000

14._____

Write in ordinary notation:

15. 6.5×10^4

15._____

16. 4.76×10^{-2}

16._____

Calculate using scientific notation and rules of exponents.
Write your answer in scientific notation.

17. $(0.000023)(40,000,000,000)$

17._____

18. $\dfrac{(88,000,000)}{(0.00002)(0.00011)}$

18._____

Answers

Chapter 5 Review Sheet

1. $\dfrac{1}{x^4}$ 2. $9x^2y^6$ 3. $\dfrac{4a^{10}}{b^6}$ 4. $\dfrac{1}{b^6}$ 5. x^9 6. $\dfrac{4}{y^6}$ 7. $\dfrac{z^4}{16w^4}$ 8. 1 9. $-3x^6$ 10. $2z^5$

11. $\dfrac{125}{-8}$ 12. $\dfrac{8}{27}c^6$ 13. 6.57×10^{11} 14. 1.3×10^{-3} 15. 0.000537 16. $89{,}500{,}000$ 17. 6.3×10^6

18. 4×10^8

Chapter 5 Test

1. x^2 2. $27x^{15}y^3$ 3. $\dfrac{49b^{18}}{a^{10}}$ 4. b^6 5. x^6 6. $\dfrac{-8}{y^4}$ 7. $\dfrac{b}{a}$ 8. $25a^8b^2$ 9. $-3x^2$

10. 16 11. $16c^5$ 12. 1 13. 5.8×10^{-5} 14. 2.36×10^5 15. $65{,}000$ 16. 0.0476

17. 9.2×10^5 18. 4×10^{16}

Chapter 6 Topics

Chapter 6 Review Sheet

1. Write $5x^2 + 3x^5 - 4x + 7$ in descending order.   1._____

2. Write the name and degree of: $3x^2 - 5x + 3$ 2._____

3. Write the name and degree of: $6 - 2x$ 3._____

4. Write the name and degree of: -56 4._____

Add the polynomials:

5. $5x^3 - 3x^2 + 7x - 9$ and $12 - 4x + 11x^3$ 5._____

6. $6 + 5a^4 - 3a^2$, $12a^2 + 5a$ and $8a^3 + 4a^4 - 12$ 6._____

Subtract the polynomials:

7. $(14x^3 - 5x^2 + 3x - 9) - (-3x^3 + 5x - 15)$ 7._____

8. $(5b - 3b^3 + 6b^5 - 9b^2 + 7) - (14b^2 - 1b^5 - 10b^4 + 7)$ 8._____

9. Subtract $4x^3 - 5x + 7$ from $13x^2 - 10 + 5x^3$ 9._____

Perform the indicated operations:

10. $(3x - 5)(2x + 11)$ 10._____

11. $(-2x^2y)(-3y^3)(-4x^4y^2)$ 11._____

12. $(5 - 3x^2 + 11x^3)(-4x^4)$ 12._____

13. $(2x + 1)(x^2 - 5x + 7)$ 13._____

14. $(10x^4 - 5x^3 + 7)(x - 4)$ 14._____

15. $(16y^3 - 8y^2 + 10y - 60) \div (-2y)$ 15._____

16. $(9y^4 - 27y^3 + 18y^2 - 5) \div (9y^3)$ 16._____

17. $(x^2 - 3x + 7) \div (x - 2)$ 17._____

18. $(4x^2 - 6x + 9) \div (2x - 6)$ 18._____

19. $(x^3 - 27) \div (x - 3)$

20. $(x^4 - 5x^2 + 3x - 1) \div (x + 3)$

19._____

20._____

Chapter 6 Test

1. Write $11x^4 + 3x^9 - 2x^2 + 7$ in descending order.

1._____

2. Write the name and degree of: $4x^3 + 15x + 35$

2._____

3. Write the name and degree of: $36 - 2x^3$

3._____

4. Write the name and degree of: 12

4._____

Add the polynomials:

5. $-2x^3 + 5x^2 - 7x - 1$ and $6 - 4x + 13x^2$

5._____

6. $3 + 2a^3 - 3a^5$, $9a^2 + 3$ and $8a^2 + 4a^3 - 8a$

6._____

Subtract the polynomials:

7. $(x^3 - x^2 + 8x - 3) - (2x^3 + 10x - 5)$

7._____

8. $(b - 3b^3 - 4b^2 + 7) - (14b^2 - 1b^3 - 10b^4 + 7)$

8._____

9. Subtract $2x^2 - 3x - 7$ from $9x^2 - 5x + 1$

9._____

Perform the indicated operations:

10. $(x + 2)(5x - 4)$

10._____

11. $(4x^3y)(-7xy^3)(x^4)$

11._____

12. $(9 + x + 11x^2)(3x)$

12._____

13. $(x - 4)(2x^2 - 4x + 1)$

13._____

14. $(7x^3 - 5x + 2)(x + 5)$

14._____

15. $(49y^3 - 56y^2 + 70y - 42) \div (7y)$

15._____

16. $(15y^3 - 27y^2 + 4y - 18) \div (-3y^2)$

16._____

17. $(5x^2 - x + 2) \div (x + 1)$

17._____

18. $(9x^2 - 3x + 5) \div (3x - 2)$

18._____

19. $(x^3 + 2x^2 - 4) \div (x - 2)$ 19._____

20. $(x^4 - x^2 + 7x - 4) \div (x + 4)$ 20._____

Answers

Chapter 6 Review Sheet

1. $3x^5 + 5x^2 - 4x + 7$ 2. trinomial, degree 2   3. binomial, degree 1   4. monomial, degree 0

5. $16x^3 - 3x^2 + 3x + 3$ 6. $9a^4 + 8a^3 + 9a^2 + 5a - 6$ 7. $17x^3 - 5x^2 - 2x + 6$

8. $7b^5 + 10b^4 - 3b^3 - 23b^2 + 5b$ 9. $13x^2 - 17 + x^3 + 5x$ 10. $6x^2 + 23x - 55$ 11. $-24x^6y^6$

12. $-20x^4 + 12x^6 - 44x^7$ 13. $2x^3 - 9x^2 + 9x + 7$ 14. $10x^5 - 45x^4 + 20x^3 + 7x - 28$

15. $-8y^2 + 4y - 5 + 30/y$ 16. $y - 3 + 2/y - 5/(9y^3)$ 17. $x - 1$, rem. 5   18. $2x + 3$, rem. 27

19. $x^2 + 3x + 9$ 20. $x^3 - 3x^2 + 4x - 9$, rem. 26

Chapter 6 Test

1. $3x^9 + 11x^4 - 2x^2 + 7$ 2. trinomial, degree 3   3. binomial, degree 3   4. monomial, degree 0

5. $-2x^3 + 18x^2 - 11x + 5$ 6. $6a^3 - 3a^5 + 17a^2 - 8a + 6$ 7. $-x^3 - x^2 - 2x + 2$

8. $10b^4 - 2b^3 - 18b^2 + b$ 9. $7x^2 - 2x + 8$ 10. $5x^2 + 6x - 8$ 11. $-28x^8y^4$

12. $27x + 3x^2 + 33x^3$ 13. $2x^3 - 12x^2 + 17x - 4$ 14. $7x^4 + 35x^3 - 5x^2 - 23x + 10$

15. $7y^2 - 8y + 10 - 6/y$ 16. $-5y + 9 - 4/(3y) + 6/(y^2)$ 17. $5x - 6$, rem. 8   18. $3x + 1$, rem. 7

19. $x^2 + 4x + 8$, rem. 12   20. $x^3 - 4x^2 + 15x - 53$, rem. 208

Chapter 7 Topics

Chapter 7 Review Sheet

Find the product .

1. $(x - 3)(x + 7)$ 1._____

2. $(2x - 1)(3x + 4)$ 2._____

3. $(5x - 3)(2x + 1)$ 3._____

4. $(9x - 1)^2$ 4._____

Factor completely. If not factorable, write prime.

5. $-27x^4y^2 - 24x^3y^5 + 30x^5y^3$ 5._____

6. $7a + 15a^4$ 6._____

7. $21x^5y^2 + 14x^6y^2$ 7._____

8. $x^2 + 4x - 5$ 8._____

9. $x^2 - 9x + 8$ 9._____

10. $a^2 + 12a + 27$ 10._____

11. $y^2 + 3y - 5$ 11._____

12. $3x^2 + x - 2$ 12._____

13. $7y^2 - 15y + 2$ 13._____

14. $y^2 - 900$ 14._____

15. $16a^2 - 49b^2$ 15._____

16. $5x^2 + 10x - 5$ 16._____

17. $2x^2 + 5xy - 4y^2$ 17._____

18. $36x^2 - 64y^2$ 18._____

19. $25x^2 + 16$ 19._____

20. $3a^3 + 15a^2 - 18a$ 20._____

Chapter 7 Test

Find the product .

1. $(x + 5)(x + 4)$

2. $(4x + 3)(2x - 1)$

3. $(7x - 9)(x - 4)$

4. $(x + 7)^2$

1._____

2._____

3._____

4._____

Factor completely. If not factorable, write prime.

5. $12x^3y - 15x^2y^3 + 40x^5y^2$

6. $15x^3y^4 - 20x^3y^3$

7. $4a^5 - 12a^2$

8. $x^2 - 3x + 2$

9. $x^2 + 7x - 8$

10. $a^2 + 13a + 42$

11. $y^2 + y + 2$

12. $2x^2 - x + 15$

13. $4y^2 + 9$

14. $4y^2 + 25y - 21$

15. $25a^2 - 4b^2$

16. $3x^2 - 9x - 12$

17. $x^2 + 3xy - 10y^2$

18. $x^2 - 144$

19. $100x^2 - 25y^2$

20. $4a^3 - 12a^2 + 8a$

5._____

6._____

7._____

8._____

9._____

10._____

11._____

12._____

13._____

14._____

15._____

16._____

17._____

18._____

19._____

20._____

Answers

Chapter 7 Review Sheet

1. $x^2 + 4x - 21$ 2. $6x^2 + 5x - 4$ 3. $10x^2 - x - 3$ 4. $81x^2 - 18x + 1$

5. $3x^3y^2(-9x - 8y^3 + 10x^2y)$ 6. $a(7 + 15a^3)$ 7. $7x^5y^2(3 + 2x)$ 8. $(x - 1)(x + 5)$

9. $(x - 8)(x - 1)$ 10. $(a + 9)(a + 3)$ 11. prime   12. $(3x - 2)(x + 1)$ 13. $(7y - 1)(x - 2)$

14. $(y - 30)(y + 30)$ 15. $(4a - 7b)(4a + 7b)$ 16. $5(x + 3)(x - 1)$ 17. $(2x - y)(x + 4y)$

18. $4(3x - 4y)(3x + 4y)$ 19. prime   20. $3a(a + 6)(a - 1)$

Chapter 7 Test

1. $x^2 + 9x + 20$ 2. $8x^2 + 2x - 3$ 3. $7x^2 - 37x + 36$ 4. $x^2 + 14x + 49$

5. $x^2y(12x - 15y^2 + 40x^3y)$ 6. $5x^3y^3(3y - 4)$ 7. $4a^2(a^3 - 3)$ 8. $(x - 2)(x - 1)$

9. $(x + 8)(x - 1)$ 10. $(a + 6)(a + 7)$ 11. prime   12. $(2x + 5)(x - 3)$ 13. prime

14. $(4x - 3)(x + 7)$ 15. $(5a - 2b)(5a + 2b)$ 16. $3(x + 1)(x - 4)$ 17. $(x - 2y)(x + 5y)$

18. $(x - 12)(x + 12)$ 19. $25(2x - y)(2x + y)$ 20. $4a(a - 2)(a - 1)$

Chapter 8 Topics

Chapter 8 Review Sheet

For what value(s) of x is the fraction not defined?

1. $\dfrac{3}{2x - 1}$

2. $\dfrac{x + 1}{x^2 - 4x + 3}$

Find the missing term using the rule for signs for fractions:

3. $\dfrac{5}{-6} = \dfrac{-5}{?}$

4. $\dfrac{4}{2 - x} = \dfrac{-4}{?}$

Reduce to lowest terms:

5. $\dfrac{6x + 2}{9x^2 - 1}$

6. $\dfrac{x^2 + 5x + 4}{6x^2 - 6}$

7. $\dfrac{x^3 - 7x^2 - 10x}{6x^2 - 6}$

Perform the indicated operations. Reduce to lowest terms.

8. $\dfrac{x - 3}{5y^2} \cdot \dfrac{25xy^3}{4x - 12}$

9. $\dfrac{10x - 15}{x^2 + 25} \div \dfrac{4x^2 - 9}{x^2 - 5x - 6}$

10. $\dfrac{6x + 3y}{x - 2y} - \dfrac{x + 15y}{x - 2y}$

11. $\dfrac{3}{5 - x} + \dfrac{4x}{x - 5}$

12. $\dfrac{3}{4x} - 2x$

1._____

2._____

3._____

4._____

5._____

6._____

7._____

8._____

9._____

10._____

11._____

12._____

13. $\dfrac{5}{x^2 - 3x + 2} - \dfrac{2}{2x^2 - 8}$

14. $\dfrac{4x - 20}{x^2 - 6x - 27} \div \dfrac{x^3 - 25x}{x^4 - 81x^2}$

13._____

14._____

Simplify:

15. $\dfrac{\dfrac{1}{a^2} - \dfrac{2}{a} + 1}{\dfrac{a - 1}{a}}$

15._____

16. $\dfrac{\dfrac{1}{x - 3} - \dfrac{4}{x^2 - 9}}{\dfrac{2}{x + 3} + \dfrac{x}{x^2 - 9}}$

16._____

Solve and check:

17. $\dfrac{1}{x} - \dfrac{2}{4x} = \dfrac{1}{5}$

18. $\dfrac{2}{x - 4} + 5 = \dfrac{-10}{20 - 5x}$

17._____

18._____

19. $\dfrac{-1}{1 - 3x} - \dfrac{2x}{9x^2 - 1} = \dfrac{5}{9x^2 - 1}$

19._____

20. A number minus five is divided by two. The result is twice the number plus three. Find the number.

20._____

Chapter 8 Test

For what value(s) of x is the fraction not defined?

1. $\dfrac{5x}{x+2}$

2. $\dfrac{3x-2}{x^2-9}$

Find the missing term using the rule for signs for fractions:

3. $-\dfrac{3}{4} = \dfrac{?}{-4}$

4. $\dfrac{5}{x-1} = \dfrac{?}{1-x}$

Reduce to lowest terms:

5. $\dfrac{3x-3}{x^2-1}$

6. $\dfrac{x^2-4}{x^2-3x+2}$

7. $\dfrac{x^2+3x-2}{x^2+7x-10}$

Perform the indicated operations. Reduce to lowest terms.

8. $\dfrac{4x}{x-y} \cdot \dfrac{2x-2y}{10x^3}$

9. $\dfrac{x^2-36}{x+3} \div \dfrac{x^2-7x+6}{7x+21}$

10. $\dfrac{3x-2}{x+1} + \dfrac{2x+7}{x+1}$

11. $\dfrac{2a}{a-1} - \dfrac{3}{1-a}$

12. $4 - \dfrac{1}{2x}$

1._____

2._____

3._____

4._____

5._____

6._____

7._____

8._____

9._____

10._____

11._____

12._____

13. $\dfrac{1}{x^2 - 9} + \dfrac{4}{x^2 + 2x - 3}$

13._____

14. $\dfrac{3x + 15}{x^2 - 49} \cdot \dfrac{7x + 49}{x^2 - 25}$

14._____

Simplify:

15. $\dfrac{\dfrac{1}{x} - \dfrac{x}{2}}{\dfrac{5}{x}}$

15._____

16. $\dfrac{\dfrac{5}{x^2 - 1}}{\dfrac{1}{x + 1} + \dfrac{3}{x - 1}}$

16._____

Solve and check:

17. $\dfrac{1}{2} - \dfrac{1}{x} = \dfrac{2}{3}$

17._____

18. $\dfrac{1}{x + 3} - 2 = \dfrac{1}{x + 3}$

18._____

19. $\dfrac{4x - 6}{x^2 - 1} + \dfrac{1}{x + 1} = \dfrac{1}{x - 1}$

19._____

20. Two thirds is the same as one quarter less than one over a number. Find the number.

20._____

Answers

Chapter 8 Review Sheet

1. $\dfrac{1}{2}$ 2. 3, 1   3. 6   4. $x - 2$ 5. $\dfrac{2}{3x - 1}$ 6. $\dfrac{x + 4}{6(x - 1)}$ 7. can't reduce

8. $\dfrac{5xy}{4}$ 9. $\dfrac{5(x - 6)(x + 1)}{(x^2 + 25)(2x + 3)}$ 10. $\dfrac{5x - 12y}{x - 2y}$ 11. $\dfrac{4x - 3}{x - 5}$ 12. $\dfrac{-8x^2 + 3}{4x}$

13. $\dfrac{4x + 5}{(x - 2)(x - 1)(x + 2)}$ 14. $\dfrac{4x(x + 9)}{(x + 3)(x + 5)}$ 15. $\dfrac{a - 1}{a}$ 16. $\dfrac{x - 1}{3x - 6}$

17. $\dfrac{5}{2}$ 18. no solution   19. 4   20. $-\dfrac{1}{3}$

Chapter 8 Test

1. -2   2. 3, -3   3. 3   4. -5   5. $\dfrac{3}{x + 1}$ 6. $\dfrac{x + 2}{x - 1}$ 7. can't reduce

8. $\dfrac{4}{5x^2}$ 9. $\dfrac{7(x + 6)}{x - 1}$ 10. 5   11. $\dfrac{2a + 3}{a - 1}$ 12. $\dfrac{8x - 1}{2x}$

13. $\dfrac{5x - 3}{(x - 3)(x + 3)(x - 1)}$ 14. $\dfrac{21}{(x - 7)(x - 5)}$ 15. $\dfrac{2 - x^2}{10}$ 16. $\dfrac{5}{4x + 2}$

17. -6   18. no solution   19. 2   20. 12/11

Chapter 9 Topics

Chapter 9 Review Sheet

Draw a set of axes, label them properly, and locate the given points.

1. (-3, 6)

2. (1, -2.5)

3. (-1, 0)

Give the ordered pair which represents each point on the graph, and tell in which quadrant it is located.

4. A (,)   4._____

5. B (,)   5._____

6. C (,)   6._____

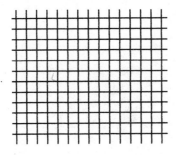

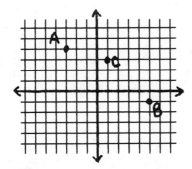

Graph each of the following equations:

7. y = -2x + 5

8. 3x - 4y = 8

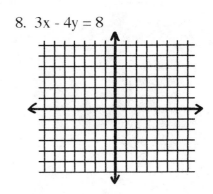

45

Find the slope of the line containing the given points:

9. (4, -6) , (-8, 0)

9._____

10. (6, -2) , (-3, -2)

10._____

11. (-8, 3) , (-2, -6)

11._____

Find the slope and y-intercept of the line with the following equations:

12. $y = -\frac{1}{4}x + 5$

12._____

13. $x - 3y = 4$

13._____

14. $x = -3$

14._____

15. $y = 0$

15._____

Write the equation of the line with the given slope which passes through the given point.

16. (-3, 4), m = -1

16._____

17. (-3, -1), m = 1/3

17._____

18. (4, 6), m is undefined

18._____

Write the equation of the line containing the two points:

19. (-2, 5), (4, -7)

19._____

20. (-2, 4), (-12, -1)

20._____

21. (5, -3), (5, 4)

21._____

Tell whether the following pairs of lines are parallel, perpendicular, or neither.

22. $2x - y = 3$
    $5x + 10y = 10$

22._____

23. $3x + 2y = 6$
    $3x - y = -2$

23._____

24. $x + 2y = -3$
    $5 + x = -2y$

24._____

25. Write the equation of any line perpendicular to $y - 3x = 4$

25._____

26. Write the equation of a line which passes through the point
    (-3, 5) and has no x-intercept.

26._____

27. Write the equation of a vertical line containing the
    point (-4, 6).

27._____

28. Write the equation of the horizontal line containing the
    point (-2, -1).

28._____

29. The Sudsy Scrubber Washing Machine Company can
    produce 4 machines at a cost of $1000 in one day. If the
    company can produce 8 machines in a day, the cost is $1500.
    The relationship between the number of machines produced,
    and the cost is linear. Write an equation expressing this
    relationship.

29._____

Graph using slope and y-intercept.

30. $y = -3x + 4$

31. $2x - 2y = 6$

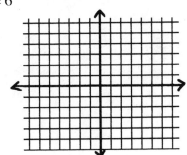

32. $y = \frac{1}{2}x - 3$

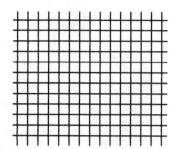

33. $y = -\frac{3}{4}x + 1$

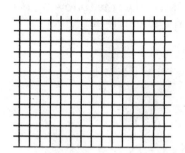

Graph the given inequalities:

34. $y \geq -3x + 2$

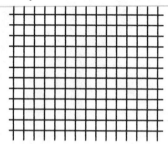

35. $y < -3$

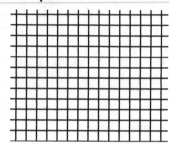

Chapter 9 Test

Draw a set of axes, label them properly, and locate the given points.

1. (0, 4)

2. (1.5, -2)

3. (-3, -2)

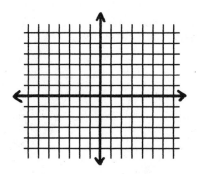

Give the ordered pair which represents each point on the graph, and tell in which quadrant it is located.

4. A (,)

5. B (,)

6. C (,)

4._____

5._____

6._____

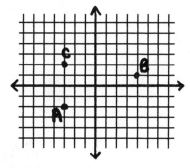

Graph each of the following equations:

7. $y = 2x - 3$

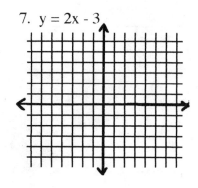

8. $-2x + 3y = -9$

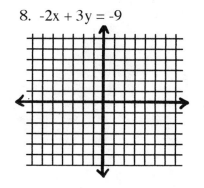

Find the slope of the line containing the given points:

9. (0, -5) , (4, -3)

9._____

10. (-2, 4) , (-5, -3)

10._____

11. (5, 1) , (-2, 1)

11._____

Find the slope and y-intercept of the line with the following equations:

12. $y = \frac{2}{3}x - 4$

12._____

13. $y - 2x = 7$

13._____

14. $y = -5$

14._____

15. $x = 4$

15._____

Write the equation of the line with the given slope which passes through the given point.

16. (-5, 0), m = -1

16._____

17. (6, -4), m = 1/3

17._____

18. (-2, -1), m is undefined

18._____

Write the equation of the line containing the two points:

19. (-3, 2), (-2, -3)

19._____

20. (3, -4), (-6, -4)

20._____

21. (1, -3), (-7, 1)

21._____

Tell whether the following pairs of lines are parallel, perpendicular, or neither.

22. $3x - y = -2$
    $x + 3y = 6$

22._____

23. $-3x + 6y = 1$
    $x - 2y = 4$

23._____

24. $2x + y = 4$
    $4x + y = -1$

24._____

25. Write the equation of any line parallel to $3x - y = 4$

25._____

26. Write the equation of a line which passes through the point (-4, -2) and has no y-intercept.

26._____

27. Write the equation of a vertical line containing the point (2,3).

27._____

28. Write the equation of the horizontal line containing the point (-5, 1).

28._____

29. The Big Dude Ranch charges each guest $100 plus $4 for each empty room at the ranch. Find the equation that relates the cost for a guest with the number of empty rooms. What will a guest pay if there are 9 empty rooms?

29._____

Graph using slope and y-intercept.

30. $y = 2x - 3$

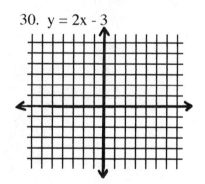

31. $3x - y = -1$

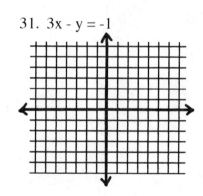

32. $y = -\frac{2}{3}x + 3$

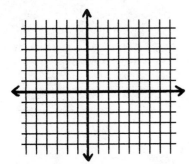

33. $y = \frac{1}{3}x - 2$

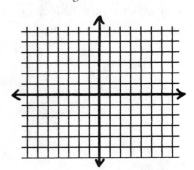

Graph the given inequalities:

34. $y < 2x - 1$

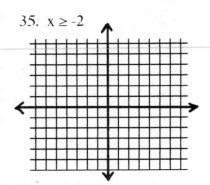

35. $x \geq -2$

Answers

Chapter 9 Review Sheet

1, 2, & 3:

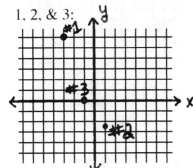

4. (-3, 4), Quadrant II   5. (5, -1), Quadrant IV   6. (1, 3), Quadrant I

7.

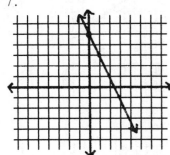

8.

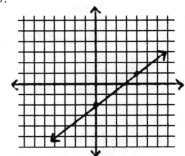

9. $-\frac{1}{2}$ 10. 0   11. $-\frac{3}{2}$ 12. m = $-\frac{1}{4}$, y-int. = 5   13. m = $\frac{1}{3}$, y-int. = $-\frac{4}{3}$ 14. m = undefined, no y-int.

15. m = 0, y-int. = 0   16. y = -x + 1   17. y = (1/3)x   18. x = 4   19. y = -2x + 1

20. y = -16x - 28   21. x = 5   22. perpendicular   23. neither   24. parallel

25. y = 3x + b, where b is any real number.   26. y = 5   27. x = -4   28. y = -1

29. y = 1000x - 2000

30.

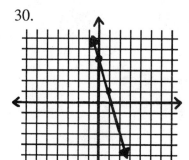

31.

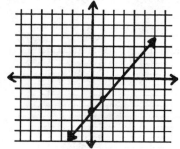

32.

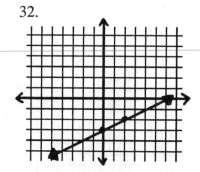

33.

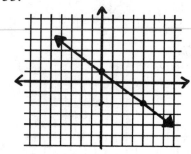

34.

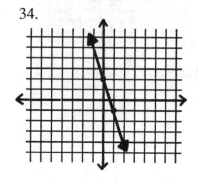

35.

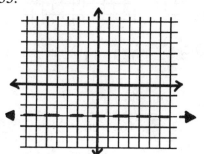

Chapter 9 Test

1, 2, & 3:

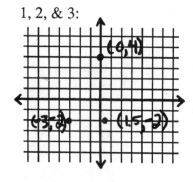

4. (-3, -2), Quadrant III   5. (4, 1), Quadrant I   6. (-3, 2), Quadrant II

7.
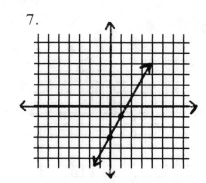

8.
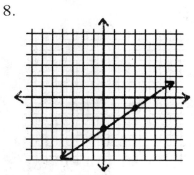

9. 1/2   10. 3/7   11. undefined   12. m = 2/3, y-int. = -4   13. m = 2, y-int. = 7

14. m = 0, y-int. = -5   15. m undefined, no y-int.   16. y = -x - 5   17. y = (1/3)x - 6

18. x = -2   19. y = -5x + 17   20. y = -4   21. y = (-1/2)x - (5/2)   22. perpendicular

23. parallel   24. neither   25. y = 3x + b, where b is any real number   26. x = -4

27. x = 2   28. y = 1   29. y = 4x + 100 , The guest will pay $136 if there are 9 empty rooms.

30.
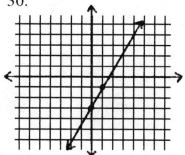

31.
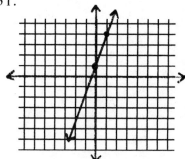

32.
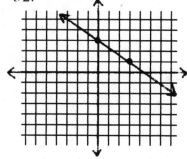

33.
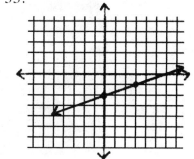

34.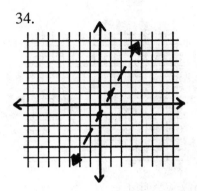

35.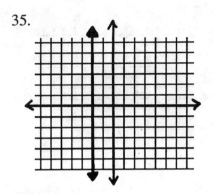

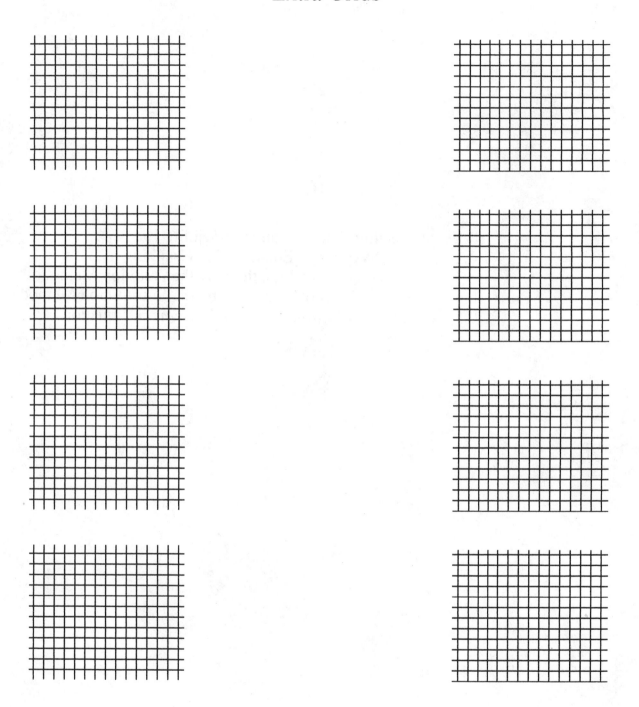

Chapter 10 Topics

Chapter 10 Review Sheet

Determine whether the given pairs of equations are intersecting, parallel, or coincident, without graphing:

1. $2x - y = 4$
    $-6x + 3y = -12$

    1._____

2. $4x = 2y - 6$
    $y - 2x = 3$

    2._____

3. $2x - 3y = -2$
    $3y = x + 4$

    3._____

Solve by graphing:

4. $y - x = 1$
    $x = 3 - y$

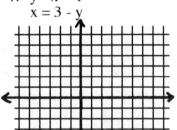

5. $y - 2x = -5$
    $2y - x = 0$

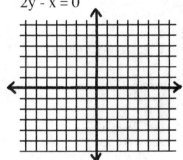

6. $x - 3y = -1$
    $2x = 6y + 1$

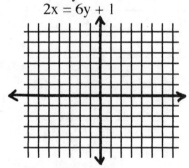

Solve using the addition method:

7. $4x - y = 5$
$x + y = -10$

7._____

8. $3x - y = 4$
$2x + 3y = -1$

8._____

9. $2x + 3y = 5$
$5x - 2y = 1$

9._____

10. $2x - 4y = -1$
$-3x + 6y = 2$

10._____

Solve using the substitution method:

11. $x - 3y = 5$
$2x + y = -1$

11._____

12. $y = -3x$
$2x - 4y = 28$

12._____

Solve using any method:

13. $y = -2$
$3x - 4y = 5$

13._____

14. $4x - 2y = 16$
$-6x + 3y = -2$

14._____

15. The sum of two numbers is 49. One number is 7 more than twice the other number. Find both numbers.

15._____

16. The perimeter of a rectangular corn field is 960 meters. If the length of the field is three times the width, find the dimensions of the field.

16._____

17. A collection of 17 dimes and nickels totals $1.35. How many of each coin are there?

17._____

18. Carnations cost $5 per dozen, and roses $12 per dozen. The two flowers are mixed to form a bouquet which costs $8 per dozen. If there are 21 flowers in the bouquet, how many roses and carnations were used?

18._____

19. Rufus is twice as old as Dweezel. Seven years ago, Dweezel   19._____
was 11 years less than three times Rufus' age. How old are
Rufus and Dweezel?

20. Peach nectar sells for $7 a pint, and orange juice sells for $3   20._____
a pint. A 16 pint mixture of the nectar and juice sells for $80.
How many pints of peach nectar and orange juice were used?

Chapter 10 Test

Determine whether the given pairs of equations are intersecting, parallel, or coincident, without graphing:

1. $x - 4y = 6$
    $4y = 3x - 2$

1._____

2. $3y = x + 2$
    $2x - 6y = 4$

2._____

3. $x - 3y = 2$
    $-4x = 7 - 12y$

3._____

Solve by graphing:

4. $y + 2x = 2$
    $y - 2 = 0$

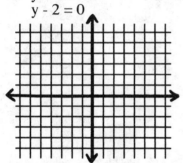

5. $x + y = 0$
    $y - x = -2$

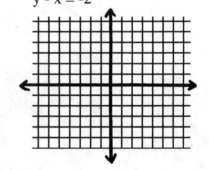

6. $3x + 6y = -9$
    $-2x - 4y = 6$

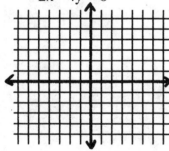

Solve using the addition method:

7. $x + 3y = 5$
    $-x + y = 3$

7._____

8. $x - 5y = -2$
    $-2x + 3y = -10$

8._____

9. $4x - 6y = 2$
    $-2x + 3y = -1$

9._____

10. $4x - 3y = -5$
    $2x + 5y = 4$

10._____

Solve using the substitution method:

11. $4x + y = 1$
    $x - y = -3$

11._____

12. $3x - 2y = -10$
    $x = 4y$

12._____

Solve using any method:

13. $-2x + 3y = 3$
    $4x - 6y = -10$

13._____

14. $4x + 3y = 1$
    $x = -2$

14._____

15. The sum of two numbers is 47. One number is 3 less than four times the other number. Find both numbers.

15._____

16. The perimeter of a rectangular pumpkin field is 450 yards. If the length of the field is twice the width, find the dimensions of the field.

16._____

17. A collection of 14 quarters and nickels totals $2.70. How many of each coin are there?

17._____

18. Big Belly pumpkin seeds cost $2.30 per cup. Snazzy Orange pumpkin seeds cost $5.20 per cup. If a mixture of 58 cups of both types of seeds sells for $243.60, how many cups of each type of seed was used?

18._____

19. Pam is three times as old as Kyra. Three years ago, Pam was six times older than Kyra. How old are Kyra and Pam now?

19._____

20. Wild Chicadee Bird Seed costs $10 per kilogram. Tame Bluebird Bird Seed costs $15 per kilogram. A mixture of both seeds is sold in a 5 kilogram bag for $60. How much of each type of seed is in the bag?

20._____

Answers

Chapter 10 Review Sheet

1. intersecting   2. coincident   3. intersecting

4.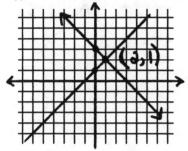

5.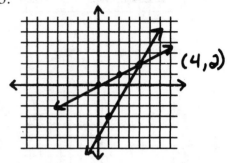

6.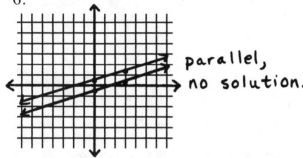
parallel, no solution.

7. (-1, -9)   8. (1, -1)   9. (13/19, 23/19)   10. no solution   11. (1/4, -3/2)   12. (2, -6)

13. (-1, -2)   14. no solution   15. 14 and 35   16. 120 m by 360 m   17. 10 dimes, 7 nickels

18. 9 roses, 12 carnations   19. Dweezel 5 years, Rufus 10 years

20. 8 pints peach nectar, 8 pints orange juice

Chapter 10 Test

1. intersecting   2. parallel   3. parallel

4.
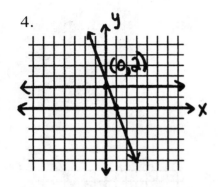

5.
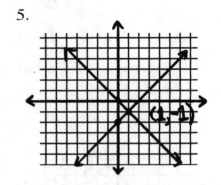

6.
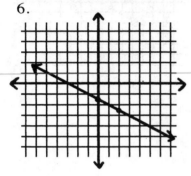

coincident, infinite number of solutions.

7. (-1, 2)   8. (8, 2)   9. infinite number of solutions   10. (-1/2, 1)   11. (-2/5, 13/5)

12. (-4, -1)   13. no solution   14. (-2, 3)   15. 10, 37   16. 85 yards, 170 yards

17. 10 quarters, 4 nickels   18. 20 cups Big Belly seeds, 38 cups Snazzy Orange seeds

19. Kyra 15 years, Pam 45 years   20. 2 kg Tame Bluebird seed, 3 kg Wild Chicadee seed

Chapter 11 Topics

Chapter 11 Review Sheet

Evaluate if possible:

1. $\sqrt{81}$

              1._____

2. $\sqrt{-81}$

              2._____

3. $-\sqrt{81}$

              3._____

Indicate which of the following are rational or irrational:

4. 2π

              4._____

5. $1.61161116\ldots$

              5._____

6. $\dfrac{12}{7}$

              6._____

7. $43.2323\ldots$

              7._____

Simplify the following:

8. $\sqrt{40x^2}$

              8._____

9. $\sqrt{72a^7b^4}$

              9._____

Multiply and simplify:

10. $\sqrt{14}\ \sqrt{21}$

              10._____

11. $\sqrt{x^9}\ \sqrt{x^4}$

              11._____

Simplify, and combine if possible:

12. $4\sqrt{3} - 3\sqrt{3}$

13. $3\sqrt{5} - 4\sqrt{10} + 6\sqrt{2}$

14. $3\sqrt{18} + 5\sqrt{50} - 4\sqrt{27}$

12._____

13._____

14._____

Divide and simplify:

15. $\dfrac{\sqrt{27}}{\sqrt{9}}$

16. $\sqrt{\dfrac{100}{36}}$

17. $\dfrac{\sqrt{28x^5}}{\sqrt{7x}}$

15._____

16._____

17._____

Rationalize the denominator and simplify:

18. $\dfrac{\sqrt{6}}{\sqrt{15}}$

19. $\dfrac{2\sqrt{5}}{3\sqrt{2}}$

18._____

19._____

Multiply and simplify:

20. $\sqrt{5}\,(\,3\sqrt{2}\, - 4\sqrt{10}\,)$

20._____

21. $(\,2\sqrt{5}\, - 3\sqrt{2}\,)(\,2\sqrt{5}\, + 3\sqrt{2}\,)$

21._____

22. $(\,4 - 3\sqrt{x}\,)(7 + 2\sqrt{x}\,)$

22._____

Write the conjugate:

23. $6\sqrt{7} + 3\sqrt{2}$

23._____

Rationalize and simplify:

24. $\dfrac{\sqrt{3}}{2 - \sqrt{3}}$

24._____

25. $\dfrac{1 - 3\sqrt{5}}{4 + \sqrt{5}}$

25._____

Solve and check:

26. $\sqrt{1 - 2x} = 7$

26._____

27. $5 - \sqrt{x + 3} = 6$

27._____

In the right triangle with legs a and b , and hypotenuse c, find the missing side.

28. $b = 4, c = 10$

28._____

Determine whether or not the given triangle is a right triangle.

29. $a = 3\sqrt{5}$ $b = \sqrt{6}$ $c = \sqrt{21}$

29._____

30. Find the height of a flag pole, if a 20 foot ladder reaches the tip of the pole when the base of the ladder is 12 feet from the base of the flag pole.

30._____

Chapter 11 Test

Evaluate if possible:

1. $\sqrt{100}$

2. $-\sqrt{100}$

3. $\sqrt{-100}$

1._____

2._____

3._____

Indicate which of the following are rational or irrational:

4. 1.313131 . . .

5. $-\pi$

6. $\dfrac{2}{3}$

7. 0.656656665 . . .

4._____

5._____

6._____

7._____

Simplify the following:

8. $\sqrt{75x^5}$

9. $\sqrt{45a^6b^3}$

8._____

9._____

Multiply and simplify:

10. $\sqrt{15}\,\sqrt{9}$

11. $\sqrt{x^2}\,\sqrt{x^5}$

10._____

11._____

Simplify, and combine if possible:

12. $5\sqrt{7} - \sqrt{7}$

13. $2\sqrt{20} - 3\sqrt{28} + 5\sqrt{12}$

14. $4\sqrt{5} - 2\sqrt{3} + 5\sqrt{6}$

12._____

13._____

14._____

Divide and simplify:

15. $\dfrac{\sqrt{12}}{\sqrt{3}}$

16. $\sqrt{\dfrac{81}{27}}$

17. $\dfrac{\sqrt{36x^3}}{\sqrt{9x^2}}$

15._____

16._____

17._____

Rationalize the denominator and simplify:

18. $\dfrac{\sqrt{2}}{\sqrt{5}}$

19. $\dfrac{3\sqrt{2}}{\sqrt{7}}$

18._____

19._____

Multiply and simplify:

20. $\sqrt{3}\,(\,4\sqrt{3} - \sqrt{6}\,)$

20._____

21. $(\,\sqrt{7} - \sqrt{3}\,)(\,\sqrt{7} + \sqrt{3}\,)$

21._____

22. $(\,1 - 2\sqrt{y}\,)(3 - \sqrt{y}\,)$

22._____

Write the conjugate:

23. $\sqrt{11} - 4\sqrt{3}$

23._____

Rationalize and simplify:

24. $\dfrac{4}{1 + \sqrt{5}}$

24._____

25. $\dfrac{2\sqrt{3} - 1}{\sqrt{3} - 2}$

25._____

Solve and check:

26. $\sqrt{3x + 1} = 4$

26._____

27. $7 + \sqrt{x - 2} = 3$

27._____

In the right triangle with legs a and b , and hypotenuse c, find the missing side.

28. $b = 6,\ a = 5$

28._____

74

Determine whether or not the given triangle is a right triangle.

29. $a = \sqrt{3} \quad b = 3\sqrt{2} \quad c = \sqrt{21}$

29._____

30. Find the height of a window on a building if a 25 foot ladder reaches the window, and the base of the ladder is 9 feet from the base of the building.

30._____

Answers

Chapter 11 Review Sheet

1. 9 2. undefined 3. -9 4. irrational 5. irrational 6. rational 7. rational

8. $2x\sqrt{10}$ 9. $6a^3b^2\sqrt{2a}$ 10. $7\sqrt{6}$ 11. $x^6\sqrt{x}$

12. $\sqrt{3}$ 13. can't combine 14. $22\sqrt{2}$ 15. $\sqrt{3}$ 16. $\frac{5}{2}$ 17. $2x^2$

18. $\frac{\sqrt{10}}{5}$ 19. $\frac{\sqrt{10}}{3}$ 20. $3\sqrt{10} - 20\sqrt{2}$ 21. 2 22. $28 - 13\sqrt{x} - 6x$ 23. $6\sqrt{7} - 3\sqrt{2}$ 24. $2\sqrt{3} + 3$ 25. $\frac{19 - 13\sqrt{5}}{11}$

26. $x = -24$ 27. no solution 28. $2\sqrt{21}$ 29. not a right triangle 30. 16 feet

Chapter 11 Test

1. 10 2. -10 3. undefined 4. rational 5. irrational 6. rational 7. irrational

8. $5x^2\sqrt{3x}$ 9. $3a^3b\sqrt{5b}$ 10. $3\sqrt{15}$ 11. $x^3\sqrt{x}$ 12. $4\sqrt{7}$ 13. $4\sqrt{5} - 12\sqrt{7} + 10\sqrt{3}$

14. can't combine 15. 2 16. $\sqrt{3}$ 17. $2\sqrt{x}$ 18. $\frac{\sqrt{10}}{5}$ 19. $\frac{3\sqrt{14}}{7}$

20. $12 - 3\sqrt{2}$ 21. 40 22. $3 - 7\sqrt{y} + 2y$ 23. $\sqrt{11} + 4\sqrt{3}$ 24. $-1 + \sqrt{5}$ 25. $-4 - 3\sqrt{3}$

26. $x = 5$ 27. no solution 28. $\sqrt{61}$ 29. yes 30. $\sqrt{606}$ ft

Chapter 12 Topics

Chapter 12 Review Sheet

Write in standard form and identify a, b, and c.

1. $3x - 7 = 4x - 11x^2$

    1._____

2. $\dfrac{3x}{4} - \dfrac{1}{3} = \dfrac{x^2}{6}$

    2._____

Solve and check:

3. $x^2 + 3x - 4 = 0$

    3._____

4. $2x^2 = 3 - 5x$

    4._____

5. $5x^2 = 15$

    5._____

6. $(2x + 1)^2 = 25$

    6._____

Complete the square:

7. $x^2 - 6x +$ ____ $= (x -$ ____ $)^2$

    7._____

8. $x^2 + 3x +$ ____ $= (x +$ ____ $)^2$

    8._____

Solve by completing the square:

9. $x^2 - 10x + 7 = 0$

    9._____

10. $x^2 + 3x - 2 = 0$

    10._____

Solve using the quadratic formula:

11. $x^2 + 3x - 7 = 0$

    11._____

12. $3x^2 - x - 5 = 0$

    12._____

Solve by any method:

13. $10x^2 - 50x = 0$

14. $3x^2 = 14 - 19x$

15. $x - 3 = 2\sqrt{2 - x}$

13._____

14._____

15._____

Solve the following problems:

16. A number plus its reciprocal are equal to two. Find the number.

17. The length of a rectangle is 30 feet more than twice the width. If the area is 500 square feet, find the dimensions of the field.

18. Marilyn rides her bike at 22 mph with no wind. She goes on a trip and rides 10 miles to the ocean against the wind, then rides back on the same route with the wind at her back. If the trip took one hour, find the speed of the wind.

16._____

17._____

18._____

Sketch the graph of:

19. $y = -3x^2 + 4$

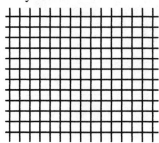

20. $y = x^2 + 3x - 4$

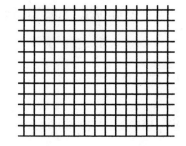

Chapter 12 Test

Write in standard form and identify a, b, and c.

1. $5x^2 - 3 = 4x + 5$

2. $\dfrac{x^2}{5} + \dfrac{3}{2} = \dfrac{x}{10}$

1._____

2._____

Solve and check:

3. $x^2 + 5x + 4 = 0$

4. $-22x = 3x^2 + 7$

5. $3x^2 = 30$

6. $(x - 2)^2 = 16$

3._____

4._____

5._____

6._____

Complete the square:

7. $x^2 + 8x +$ ____ $= (x +$ ____ $)^2$

8. $x^2 - x +$ ____ $= (x +$ ____ $)^2$

7._____

8._____

Solve by completing the square:

9. $x^2 + 6x + 3 = 0$

10. $x^2 - 5x - 4 = 0$

9._____

10._____

Solve using the quadratic formula:

11. $x^2 - 4x + 1 = 0$

12. $2x^2 + 5x - 1 = 0$

11._____

12._____

Solve by any method:

13. $8 = 2x^2 + 7x$

14. $4x^2 - 12 = 0$

15. $x + 1 = \sqrt{x + 3}$

13._____

14._____

15._____

Solve the following problems:

16. Five is equal to a number, plus four divided by a number. Find the number.

16._____

17. The length of a rectangle is 1 cm less than three times the width. If the area is 24 square feet, find the dimensions of the field.

17._____

18. Hugo rides her bike at 10 mph with no wind. She goes on a trip and rides 15 miles to the ocean against the wind, then rides back on the same route with the wind at her back. If the trip took 4 hours, find the speed of the wind.

18._____

Sketch the graph of:

19. $y = -x^2 + x + 2$

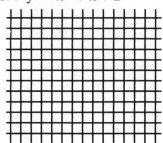

20. $y = x^2 + 2$

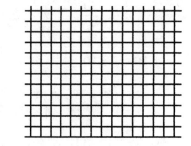

Answers

Chapter 12 Review Sheet

1. $11x^2 - x - 7 = 0$, $a = 11$, $b = -1$, $c = -7$ 2. $2x^2 - 9x + 4 = 0$, $a = 2$, $b = -9$, $c = 2$ 3. $1, -4$

4. $\frac{1}{2}, -3$ 5. $+\sqrt{3}, -\sqrt{3}$ 6. $3, 2$ 7. $9, 3$ 8. $\frac{9}{4}, \frac{3}{2}$ 9. $5 + 3\sqrt{2}, 5 - 3\sqrt{2}$

10. $-\frac{3}{2} + \frac{\sqrt{17}}{2}, -\frac{3}{2} - \frac{\sqrt{17}}{2}$ 11. $-\frac{3}{2} + \frac{\sqrt{37}}{2}, -\frac{3}{2} - \frac{\sqrt{37}}{2}$ 12. $\frac{1}{6} + \frac{\sqrt{61}}{6}, \frac{1}{6} - \frac{\sqrt{61}}{6}$

13. $0, 5$ 14. $2/3, -7$ 15. no solution   16. 1 17. 10 ft by 50 ft   18. 6.6 mph

19.

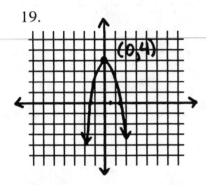

20.

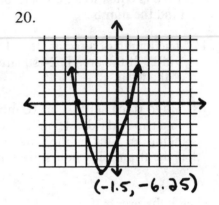

Chapter 12 Test

1. $5x^2 - 4x - 8 = 0$, $a = 5$, $b = -4$, $c = -8$ 2. $2x^2 - x + 15 = 0$, $a = 2$, $b = -1$, $c = 15$

3. $-4, -1$ 4. $-\frac{1}{3}, -7$ 5. $+\sqrt{10}, -\sqrt{10}$ 6. $6, -2$ 7. $16, 4$ 8. $\frac{1}{4}, \frac{1}{2}$

9. $-3 + \sqrt{6}, -3 - \sqrt{6}$ 10. $\frac{5}{2} + \frac{\sqrt{41}}{2}, \frac{5}{2} - \frac{\sqrt{41}}{2}$ 11. $2 + \sqrt{3}, 2 - \sqrt{3}$ 12. $-\frac{5}{4} + \frac{\sqrt{33}}{4}, -\frac{5}{4} + \frac{\sqrt{33}}{4}$

13. $-\frac{7}{4} + \frac{\sqrt{113}}{4}, -\frac{7}{4} - \frac{\sqrt{113}}{4}$ 14. $+\sqrt{3}, -\sqrt{3}$ 15. 1

16. 4 or 1   17. 8 ft by 3 ft   18. 5mph

19.

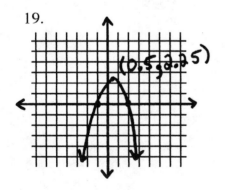

20.

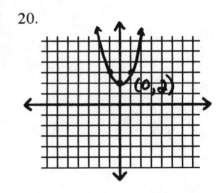

Chapter 1 Test Bank

Multiple Choice

1. Represent a bet you lose for $55 as a signed number.
   A. 55
   B. 0
   C. -55
   D. -35

   Answer: C   Section 1.1

2. Represent the temperature in Melbourne, Australia of 40° above zero as a signed number.
   A. -40°
   B. 40°
   C. 0°
   D. 30°

   Answer: B   Section 1.1

3. Find the absolute value of -3.
   A. 0
   B. 1
   C. -3
   D. 3

   Answer: D   Section 1.2

4. Find the absolute value of +2.7.
   A. 27
   B. -2.7
   C. -27
   D. 2.7

   Answer: D   Section 1.2

5. How far from zero is -25 on the number line?
   A. 25
   B. -25
   C. 0
   D. 5

   Answer: A   Section 1.2

6. Which symbol should be inserted between -27   -30 ?
   A. <
   B. >
   C. =
   D. none of the above

   Answer: B   Section 1.3

7. Which symbol should be inserted between |15| |-15| ?
    A. <
    B. >
    C. =
    D. none of the above

8. Which symbol should be inserted between 0   -4 ?
    A. <
    B. >
    C. =
    D. none of the above

9. Evaluate: -4 + 7
    A. 11
    B. 3
    C. -28
    D. -3

10. Evaluate: -15 + (-12)
    A. -27
    B. -3
    C. 3
    D. 27

11. Evaluate: -1/2 + 3/4
    A. -3/8
    B. 1/2
    C. 1/4
    D. 3/8

12. Evaluate: 14 + (-14)
    A. -28
    B. 28
    C. 0
    D. -1

13. Keesha has $37.50 in her checking account. If she deposits $23.41 and $16.30 , and writes a check for $52.13, what is her new balance?
    A. $25.08
    B. $49.92
    C. -$49.92
    D. -$25.08

14. Evaluate: 12 - (-4)
    A. 16
    B. 8
    C. -48
    D. 48

Answer: A   Section 1.5

15. Evaluate: -14 - (-10)
    A. 140
    B. -24
    C. 24
    D. -4

Answer: D   Section 1.5

16. Evaluate: 10 - 10
    A. 20
    B. 0
    C. -20
    D. -100

Answer: B   Section 1.5

17. Alisia's temperature was 103.6° F at 7:00pm. The next morning at 6:00am, her temperature
    was 101.2°F. How much did her temperature change? (Express as a signed number)
    A. 2.4°F
    B. -2.4°F
    C. 1.6°F
    D. -1.6°F

Answer: B   Section 1.5

18. Evaluate: -3 + 7 - 11 - 5 + 6
    A. 16
    B. -18
    C. 4
    D. -6

Answer: D   Section 1.6

19. Evaluate: 2.71 - 1.3 - 5.74 + 3.6
    A. 4.35
    B. -2.6
    C. -0.73
    D. 0.54

Answer: C   Section 1.6

20. Emily Louise is on a diet. Over 7 weeks, she gains and loses the following number of pounds: -3, +2.5, -1, -1.5, -2, +1.5, -2. What was her overall gain or loss?
   A. +0.5
   B. -0.5
   C. -5.5
   D. -3.5

   Answer: C Section 1.6

21. Evaluate: (-20)(3)
   A. -50
   B. 50
   C. -60
   D. 60

   Answer: C Section 1.7

22. Evaluate: (-2/3)(9/20)
   A. -3/10
   B. 3/10
   C. 40/27
   D. -40/27

   Answer: A Section 1.7

23. Evaluate: (23)(-2)(14)(0)
   A. 644
   B. -644
   C. 35
   D. 0

   Answer: D Section 1.7

24. Sing Tao bought 200 baby dolls for ten dollars a piece. She couldn't sell the dolls and sold them to a store for eight dollars a piece. How much money did she lose? Represent your answer as a signed number.
   A. $400
   B. -$400
   C. $1600
   D. -$1600

   Answer: B Section 1.7

25. Evaluate: $-33 \div 3$
   A. -99
   B. 99
   C. -11
   D. 11

   Answer: C Section 1.8

26. Evaluate: -3/4 ÷ -27/2
    A. 1/18
    B. -1/18
    C. 2/3
    D. -2/3

Answer: A   Section 1.8

27. Three college roommates owe the electric company $255. How much will each person have to pay if the bill is divided evenly?
    A. $127.50
    B. $113.00
    C. $255.00
    D. $85.00

Answer: D   Section 1.8

28. What property does $2(3 + 7) = 2(3) + 2(7)$ represent?
    A. Commutative
    B. Associative
    C. Distributive
    D. none of the above

Answer: C   Section 1.9

29. What property does $3x = x(3)$ represent?
    A. Commutative
    B. Associative
    C. Distributive
    D. none of the above

Answer: A   Section 1.9

30. What property does $c/d = d/c$ represent?
    A. Commutative
    B. Associative
    C. Distributive
    D. none of the above

Answer: D   Section 1.9

31. Evaluate: $(-1)^4$
    A. -4
    B. 1
    C. -1
    D. 4

Answer: B   Section 1.10

87

32. Evaluate: $(-10)^3$
   A. 100
   B. 1000
   C. -1000
   D. -100

   Answer: C   Section 1.10

33. Evaluate $-\sqrt{25}$

   A. -5
   B. 5
   C. -25
   D. 25

   Answer: A   Section 1.10

34. Evaluate $\sqrt[3]{-27}$
   A. 9
   B. -9
   C. 3
   D. -3

   Answer: D   Section 1.10

35. Evaluate: $5(10 - 17)$
   A. 35
   B. -35
   C. 135
   D. -135

   Answer: B   Section 1.11

36. Evaluate: $(2(3^2) - 10) \div (-4)$
   A. 4
   B. -4
   C. 2
   D. -2

   Answer: D   Section 1.11

37. Evaluate: $3 - 2[4 + (5 - 6)]$
   A. -3
   B. 3
   C. 4
   D. -4

   Answer: A   Section 1.12

38. Evaluate: $10 - [\, 6(2)^2 - (3 + 6)\,]$
    A. 2
    B. -2
    C. 5
    D. -5

Answer: D   Section 1.12

Problems

Section 1.1

Draw a number line and locate the following points:
39. -7
40. 4.8
41. 0

42. Represent twenty degrees below zero as a signed number.

43. Represent the freezing point of water, which is 32°F as a signed number.

44. Represent a mountain which is 2500 feet above sea level as a signed number.

Section 1.2

45. Find the absolute value of + 45

46. Find the absolute value of: $-\frac{2}{3}$

47. Find the absolute value of 0

48. What is the distance between -30 and 0 on the number line?

49. How far from zero is -1.7 on the number line?

Section 1.3

For problems 50 - 53, insert < > = between the following numbers to make the statement true.
50. 14   - 20

51. $2\frac{1}{2}$ $2\frac{1}{4}$

52. | - 20 | | 20 |

53. -2.3   -2.5

54. You are at mile 47 on the Garden Parkway. If there are gas stations at mile 59 and mile 33, which is closer to you?

55. What temperature is closer to zero, -15° or 12° ?

Section 1.4

56. Evaluate: $10 + 23$

57. Evaluate: $-6 + 14$

58. Evaluate: $12 + (-23)$

59. Evaluate: $-14.76 + (-5.3)$

60. Evaluate: $-13 + 0$

61. Evaluate: $\frac{2}{3} + \left(-\frac{1}{4}\right)$

62. Evaluate: $-26 + 26$

63. Darryle dives to 30 feet below sea level, and Margaret climbs to 240 feet above sea level. How far apart are Margaret and Darryle?

64. The stock if Baby Boon Company is worth 43.5 points. If the stock drops 3.25 points and increases 2.3 points, what is the current value of Baby Boon stocks?

Section 1.5

65. Evaluate: $-3 - 14$

66. Evaluate: $20 - 5$

67. Evaluate: $-2.3 - 5.6$

68. Evaluate: $426 - 513$

69. Evaluate: $-\frac{2}{3} - \left(-\frac{1}{4}\right)$

70. Evaluate: $14 - (-14)$

71. Maurice has $43.50 in his checking account. If he writes a check for $51.20, what is his new balance?

Section 1.6

72. Evaluate: $14 - (-4) - 12 + 14 - 5$

73. Evaluate: $6 - 3 + 11 - (-5) - 4 + 7$

74. Evaluate: $-\dfrac{1}{2} + \dfrac{2}{3} - \dfrac{1}{4} - \left(-\dfrac{1}{4}\right)$

75. Brandon writes checks for $13.70, $4.23, and $15.60. He deposits $2.53, $14.20 and $25.60. If his original balance was $102.41, what is his current balance?

76. The temperature changes in Toulon for the week of January 5th through 12th are as follows: -3°, +5°, -10°, +7°, +2°, -3°, -2°. What is the overall change in temperature for the week?

Section 1.7

77. Evaluate: $(-3)(-2)$

78. Evaluate: $4(-7)$

79. Evaluate: $(-1.6)(-3)$

80. Evaluate: $(-1)(2)(-3)(-4)$

81. Evaluate: $\left(-2\dfrac{1}{2}\right)\left(3\dfrac{3}{8}\right)$

82. To buy a couch on a payment plan, Marvin must pay $55 a month for 18 months. How much does the couch cost Marvin?

83. Nicki bought 400 shares of stock at $54. If she sold them for $48, find the loss and express as a signed number.

Section 1.8

84. Evaluate: $42 \div (-7)$

85. Evaluate: $0 \div (-12)$

86. Evaluate: $14 \div 0$

87. Evaluate: $(-24) \div (-3)$

88. Evaluate: $2\dfrac{1}{3} \div \left(-1\dfrac{3}{4}\right)$

89. Steve lost 28 pounds in seven weeks. What was his average weight loss per week? Express your answer as a signed number.

90. Cable TV costs $304.80 per year. How much does a cable subscriber have to pay for one month?

Section 1.9

For problems 91 through 94, state if the commutative, associative, distributive, or none of these properties is demonstrated.

91. $-3(1 + 4) = -3(5)$

92. $4(-6) = (-6)(4)$

93. $(1 + x) + 5 = 1 + (x + 5)$

94. $4 + (-10) = -10 + 4$

Section 1.10

95. Evaluate: $(-2)^3$

96. Evaluate: 5^2

97. Evaluate: $(-0.6)^2$

98. Evaluate: $\sqrt{64}$

99. Evaluate: $\sqrt[3]{8}$

100. Evaluate: $-\sqrt[5]{-1}$

Section 1.11

101. Evaluate: $4 - 3(2)$

102. Evaluate: $3 - 15 \div 5(3)$

103. Evaluate: $4^2 + 3(-2)$

104. Evaluate: $-12 - 3(-120)(0) + 15$

Section 1.12

105. Evaluate: $2[\, 5 - 2(7 - 10)\,]$

106. Evaluate: $2 + 3[\, 5 - (7 - 4)\,]$

107. Evaluate: $\{\, 6 - [4 + 2(3 - 5)] + 2\, \}$

Answers

Chapter 1 Problems

42. -20°   43. +32°   44. +2500   45. 45   46. 2/3   47. 0   48. 30   49. 1.7   50. >

51. >   52. =   53. >   54. The gas station at mile 59 is closer.   55. 12°   56. 33   57. 8

58. -11   59. -20.06   60. -13   61. 5/12   62. 0   63. 270 feet   64. 42.55   65. -17

66. 15   67. -7.9   68. -87   69. -5/12   70. 28   71. -$7.70   72. 15   73. 22   74. 1/6

75. 111.21   76. -4°   77. 6   78. -28   79. 4.8   80. -24   81. -135/16 or -8 7/16

82. $990   83. -$2400   84. -6   85. 0   86. undefined   87. 8   88. -4/3   89. -4 pounds

90. $25.40   91. none   92. commutative   93. associative   94. commutative   95. -8

96. 25   97. 0.36   98. 8   99. 2   100. 1   101. -2   102. -6   103. 10   104. 3   105. 22

106. 8   107. 8

Chapter 2 Test Bank

Multiple Choice

1. Evaluate: $A = \pi r^2$ $r = 10cm$, $\pi = 3.14$
   A. 31.4 cm^2
   B. 31.4 cm
   C. 314 cm^2
   D. 314 cm

   Answer: C   Section 2.1

2. Evaluate: $S = \frac{1}{2}gt^2$ $g = 32$, $t = 10$
   A. 1600
   B. 160
   C. 3200
   D. 320

   Answer: A   Section 2.1

3. Evaluate: $R = \frac{ab}{a+b}$ $a = 200$, $b = 800$
   A. 120
   B. 140
   C. 100
   D. 160

   Answer: D   Section 2.1

4. An astronaut who is standing on the moon throws a moonrock upward. The height, in feet, of the rock is given by: $S = -3t^2 + 30t + 5$. Find the height of a rock after t = 10seconds.
   A. 275 feet
   B. 5 feet
   C. 25 feet
   D. 125 feet

   Answer: B   Section 2.1

5. Evaluate: $-3x$ when $x = 5$, $y = -3$, $z = 6$
   A. -15
   B. 9
   C. -18
   B. 18

   Answer: A   Section 2.2

6. Evaluate: $4y + 5x$ when $x = 5$, $y = -3$, $z = 6$
   A. 13
   B. 5
   C. 14
   D. -5

   Answer: A   Section 2.2

7. Evaluate: $-y^2$ when $x = 5$, $y = -3$, $z = 6$
   A. -25
   B. 25
   C. -9
   D. 9

   Answer: C   Section 2.2

8. Evaluate: $3x - 2y + 5z$ when $x = 5$, $y = -3$, $z = 6$
   A. 39
   B. 25
   C. 14
   D. 51

   Answer: D   Section 2.2

9. Combine like terms: $2a + 3a - 11a$
   A. 16a
   B. 66a
   C. -5a
   D. -6a

   Answer: D   Section 2.3

10. Combine like terms: $4x - 3y + 8x + y$
    A. 9xy
    B. -96xy
    C. 12x - 2y
    D. x + 9y

    Answer: C   Section 2.3

11. Combine like terms: $4x^2 - 3x + 2x^2$
    A. $3x^2$
    B. $9x^2$
    C. $6x^2 + 3x$
    D. $6x^2 - 3x$

    Answer: D   Section 2.3

12. Combine like terms: $4x^2y - 3xy^2 + 4xy^2$
    A. $5xy^2$
    B. $4x^2y + xy^2$
    C. $4x^2y - xy^2$
    D. $x^2y + 4xy^2$

    Answer: B   Section 2.3

13. Simplify: x^2x^4
    A. x^6
    B. x^8
    C. x^2
    D. x^{-2}

    Answer: A   Section 2.4

14. Simplify: $10^4 10^7$
    A. 100^{11}
    B. 100^{28}
    C. 10^{11}
    D. 10^{28}

    Answer: C   Section 2.4

15. Simplify: $7 \cdot 7^3 7^5$
    A. 7^9
    B. 7^8
    C. 7^{15}
    D. 343

    Answer: A   Section 2.4

16. Simplify: $y^a y^{2b} y^{2a}$
    A. y^{5a}
    B. y^{4a}
    C. y^{4ab}
    D. $y^{3a + 2b}$

    Answer: D Section 2.4

17. Multiply: $(5y)(3y)$
    A. $8y$
    B. $15y$
    C. $15y^2$
    D. $8y^2$

    Answer: C Section 2.5

18. Multiply: $(-7y^2)(-3y^5)$
    A. $21y^7$
    B. $-21y^7$
    C. $21y^{10}$
    D. $-21y^{10}$

    Answer: A Section 2.5

19. Multiply: $(6x^2y^3)(-2x^4y)$
    A. $12x^8y^3$
    B. $-12x^8y^4$
    C. $12x^6y^4$
    D. $-12x^6y^4$

    Answer: D Section 2.5

20. Multiply: $(2x^2y)(3xy^3)(4x^4y)$
    A. $24x^8y^3$
    B. $24x^8y^5$
    C. $24x^7y^3$
    D. $24x^7y^5$

    Answer: D Section 2.5

21. Multiply: $5(x + y)$
    A. $5xy$
    B. $5x + y$
    C. $5x + 5y$
    D. $x + 5y$

    Answer: C Section 2.6

22. Multiply: $(6 - 2y)(-3)$
    A. $-18 - 6y$
    B. $-18 + 6y$
    C. $18 + 6y$
    D. $18 - 6y$

    Answer: B Section 2.6

23. Multiply: $-(4a - 3b + c)$
    A. $-4a + 3b - c$
    B. $4a - 3b - c$
    C. $-4a + 3b + c$
    D. $-4a - 3b - c$

    Answer: A Section 2.6

24. Multiply: $10a^2b(5ab^2 - 3b^3)$
    A. $15a^2b^2 - 13a^2b^3$
    B. $50a^2b^2 - 13a^2b^3$
    C. $15a^2b^2 - 30a^2b^3$
    D. $50a^3b^3 - 30a^2b^4$

Answer: D   Section 2.6

25. Simplify: $x - 3(x + y)$
    A. $-2x - 3y$
    B. $-3x^2 - 3y$
    C. $-2x + y$
    D. $x - 3y$

Answer: A   Section 2.7

26. Simplify: $3(a - 2b) - 5b$
    A. $-2a - 6b$
    B. $3a - 11b$
    C. $3a - 6b - 5b$
    D. $3a + 6b - 5b$

Answer: B   Section 2.7

27. Simplify: $5x - (-2x + 5)$
    A. $3x - 5$
    B. $3x + 5$
    C. $7x - 5$
    D. $7x + 5$

Answer: C   Section 2.7

28. Simplify: $4a + [-(4x - 6) - 11]$
    A. -5
    B. -17
    C. $4a - 4x - 5$
    D. $4a - 4x - 15$

Answer: C   Section 2.7

Problems

Section 2.1

29. Evaluate: $I = prt$, $p = \$2000$, $r = 0.07$, $t = 2$

30. $F = \frac{9}{5}C + 32$, $C = 30°$

31. Evaluate: $C = 2\pi r$, $\pi = 3.14$, $r = 12$ feet

32. $P = 2L + 2W$, $L = 5$ cm, $W = 8$ cm

33. Evaluate: $V = \frac{4}{3}\pi r^3$, $r = 6.2$

34. Evaluate: $D = \sqrt{x^2 + y^2}$, $x = 3$, $y = 4$

35. The temperature at the Ivory Coast on February 21 was $20°$ C. What is this temperature equivalent to in Fahrenheit (F) if $F = \frac{9}{5}C + 32$?

Section 2.2

36. Find the value of $4 - 2y$ if $x = 5$, $y = -3$, $z = 6$.

37. Find the value of $x + 6z$ if $x = 5$, $y = -3$, $z = 6$.

38. Find the value of x^2 if $x = 5$, $y = -3$, $z = 6$.

39. Find the value of $4xy - z$ if $x = 5$, $y = -3$, $z = 6$.

40. Find the value of $xy^2 + 3z$ if $x = 5$, $y = -3$, $z = 6$.

41. Find the value of $3(x+y)$ if $x = 5$, $y = -3$, $z = 6$.

42. Find the value of $-2x^2 - y$ if $x = 5$, $y = -3$, $z = 6$.

43. Find the value of $x(y - z)$ if $x = 5$, $y = -3$, $z = 6$.

Section 2.3

44. Combine like terms: $5x - 6x$.

45. Combine like terms: $3x + 10x + 4y$.

46. Combine like terms: $3xy + 2xy - 5y$.

47. Combine like terms: $3w - 10w + 7$.

48. Combine like terms: $4ab - 3b + 7a - 11ab + 5a$.

49. Combine like terms: $12y - 8y - (-6y)$

50. Combine like terms: $7x^3 + 11x^2y + 5xy^2 - 3x^2y$

51. Combine like terms: $4a - 3b + 11c - 10b + 5a - 3c$

Section 2.4

52. Simplify: y^3y

53. Simplify: w^5w^{10}

54. Simplify: 5^25^3

55. Simplify: $x^{10}x$

56. Simplify: x^ax^b

57. Simplify: x^2y^3

58. Simplify: $4a^2a^5$

59. Simplify: 6^26^6

Section 2.5

60. Multiply: $(-4x^3)(6x^2)$

61. Multiply: $(-2ab)(4ab)$

62. Multiply: $(4ab^2)(-5a^2b)$

63. Multiply: $(2ab)(5a)(-b)$

64. Multiply: $(6xy)(-4z)$

65. Multiply: $(-2ab)(-5ac^2)$

Section 2.6

66. Multiply: $-2(x - 3y)$

67. Multiply: $(a - 3b)4$

68. Multiply: $-(2x - 4y)$

69. Multiply: $-4x^2(5x^2 - 6x - 10)$

70. Multiply: $(3x^2 - 5x + 7)(-4x)$

71. Multiply: $- (14x - 3y + 11z - 2)$

Section 2.7

72. Simplify: $2y + 5(y - x)$

73. Simplify: $4a - 2(a - 3b)$

74. Simplify: $-5(3x - y) + 4x - 3y$

75. Simplify: $3x(x - 5) - 4(x^2 + 5x)$

76. Simplify: $3c + 7b - (6c + 11b)$

77. Simplify: $-5 + 3\{ 4x - 5[x - (x - 2)] \}$

Answers

Chapter 2 Problems

29. $280   30. 86° F   31. 75.36 feet   32. 26 cm   33. 997.8   34. 5   35. 68° F   36. 10

37. 41   38. 25   39. -66   40. 63   41. 6   42. -47   43. -45   44. -x   45. 13x + 4y

46. 5xy - 5y   47. -7w + 7   48. -7ab - 3b + 12a   49. 10y   50. $7x^3 + 8x^2y + 5xy^2$

51. 9a - 13b + 8c   52. y^4 53. w^{15} 54. 5^5 55. x^{11} 56. x^{a+b} 57. can't simplify

58. $4a^7$ 59. 6^8 60. $-24x^5$ 61. $-8a^2b^2$ 62. $-20a^3b^3$ 63. $-10a^2b^2$ 64. -24xyz

65. $10a^2bc^2$ 66. -2x + 6y   67. 4a - 12b   68. -2x + 4y   69. $-20x^4 + 24x^3 + 40x^2$

70. $-12x^3 + 20x^2 - 28x$ 71. -14x + 3y - 11z + 2   72. 7y - 5x   73. 2a + 6b   74. -11x + 2y

75. $-x^2 - 35x$ 76. -3c - 4b   77. 12x - 35

Chapter 3 Test Bank

Multiple Choice

1. Is 4 a solution to: $2x - 3 = 5$?
   A. yes
   B. no

2. Does -3 satisfy: $4y = 12$?
   A. yes
   B. no

                                               Answer: A   Section 3.1

3. Is -13 a solution to: $2(w - 3) = 3w + 7$?
   A. yes
   B. no

         Answer: B   Section 3.1

4. Solve: $x - 5 = 10$
   A. 5
   B. 15
   C. 2
   D. -2

         Answer: A   Section 3.1

5. Solve: $14 = x - 5$
   A. 19
   B. 9
   C. -19
   D. -9

         Answer: B   Section 3.2

6. Solve: $w - \dfrac{1}{2} = -\dfrac{3}{4}$

   A. $\dfrac{3}{8}$

   B. $-\dfrac{3}{8}$

   C. $-\dfrac{1}{4}$

   D. 1

         Answer: A   Section 3.2

7. Solve: $3x = 27$
   A. 9
   B. -9
   C. 24
   D. -24

         Answer: C   Section 3.2

         Answer: A   Section 3.3

8. Solve: $35 = -7w$
    A. 42
    B. -42
    C. 5
    D. -5

Answer: D   Section 3.3

9. Solve: $\frac{3}{5}y = -15$
    A. 9
    B. -9
    C. 25
    D. -25

Answer: D   Section 3.3

10. Solve: $-y = 14$
    A. -14
    B. 14
    C. -13
    D. 13

Answer: A   Section 3.3

11. Solve: $3x - 4 = 11$
    A. 7/3
    B. 5
    C. -3
    D. 2/3

Answer: B   Section 3.4

12. Solve: $6y + 7 = 2y - 9$
    A. -20
    B. 4
    C. -4
    D. 5

Answer: C   Section 3.4

13. Solve: $\frac{y}{3} - 4 = -2$
    A. 6
    B. -18
    C. 24
    D. -12

Answer: A   Section 3.4

14. Solve: $4(x + 5) = 3x + 2$
    A. 15
    B. -3
    C. 12
    D. -18

Answer: D   Section 3.5

15. Solve: $2(3x - 1) = 5(x - 3)$
    A. 14
    B. -17
    C. -13
    D. 30

Answer: C   Section 3.5

16. Solve: $0.2(x + 3) = 0.1x + 3.5$
    A. 41
    B. 29
    C. 34
    D. 14

Answer: B   Section 3.5

17. Solve: $\frac{2}{3}x + \frac{2}{5} = \frac{4}{3}$
    A. 2.6
    B. - 2.6
    C. 1.4
    D. -1.4

Answer: B   Section 3.5

18. Is $5x = 5(x + 3) - 4$ conditional, an identity, or a contradiction?
    A. conditional
    B. identity
    C. contradiction

Answer: C   Section 3.6

19. Is $6y - 3 = 3(2x - 1)$ conditional, an identity, or a contradiction?
    A. conditional
    B. identity
    C. contradiction

Answer: B   Section 3.6

20. Is $4 - 2x = 7(x + 3)$ conditional, an identity, or a contradiction?
    A. conditional
    B. identity
    C. contradiction

Answer: A   Section 3.6

21. Solve: $x + a = y$ for x.
    A. y/a
    B. y + a
    C. a/y
    D. y - a

Answer: D   Section 3.7

22. Solve: I = prt for t.
    A. I/(pr)
    B. I - pr
    C. I + pr
    D. Ipr

Answer: A   Section 3.7

23. Solve for x: 3(x + y) = w.
    A. 3w - y
    B. (1/3)w - y
    C. 3w + y
    D. 3wy

Answer: B   Section 3.7

24. Solve: x - 2 < 7
    A. x > 9
    B. x < 9
    C. x > 5
    D. x < 5

Answer: B   Section 3.8

25. Solve: -2x < 10
    A. x > 5
    B. x < 5
    C. x < -5
    D. x > -5

Answer: D   Section 3.8

26. Solve: 2(5 - 3y) - (2y + 4) < -2
    A. y > 1
    B. y < 1
    C. y > -1
    D. y < -1

Answer: A   Section 3.8

27. Solve: $\frac{2}{3}y \geq -4$
    A. y > -6
    B. y < -6
    C. y ≥ -6
    D. y ≤ -6

Answer: C   Section 3.8

Problems

Section 3.1

28. Is 1 a solution to: $5 - x = 7 + 3x$?

29. Is -1 a solution to: $3x - 1 = 4 - 2x$?

30. Does $y = -4$ satisfy: $-3y = 12$?

Section 3.2

31. Solve: $3 + x = -11$

32. Solve: $-4 = x + 12$

33. Solve: $4 + x = 30$

34. Solve: $6.4 + y = 3.5$

35. Solve: $-9.6 = z - 3.2$

Section 3.3

36. Solve: $-4x = 24$

37. Solve: $25 = 2x$

38. Solve: $-18 = -3y$

39. Solve: $-30 = -y$

40. Solve: $14.6 = -2x$

41. Solve: $\frac{2}{3}x = 12$

42. Solve: $\frac{-1}{3}w = 4$

43. Solve: $\frac{x}{4} = -5$

44. Solve: $-7 = \frac{y}{-3}$

Section 3.4

45. Solve: $5x - 3 = 4x + 7$

46. Solve: $4 - 3y = 2y - 6$

47. Solve: $-4x + 3 = 5x - 1$

48. Solve: $w = 3w - 9$

49. Solve: $7x - 3 = 0$

50. Solve: $\frac{1}{2}x + 2 = -6$

51. Solve: $1.3y + 7 = -5.2$

52. Solve: $-6x - 4 = 5x + 10$

Section 3.5

53. Solve: $-3(x - 4) = 2x + 7$

54. Solve: $10x = 2(x + 8)$

55. Solve: $4(x - 3) + 2(x + 1) = 3x + 4$

56. Solve: $\frac{1}{4}x + \frac{1}{3}x = -3$

57. Solve: $\frac{2}{3}w + 3 = w$

58. Solve: $\frac{1}{2}(x - 1) = \frac{2}{3}(x + 2)$

59. Solve: $\frac{y}{3} - \frac{1}{2} = \frac{3}{8}y + 1$

Section 3.6

60. Is $3x + 7 = 2(x - 4)$ conditional, an identity, or a contradiction?

61. Is $3x - 2(x + 4) = x + 7$ conditional, an identity, or a contradiction?

62. Is $4(x + 7) = 2(2x + 14)$ conditional, an identity, or a contradiction?

Section 3.7

63. Solve: $ab = c$ for b

64. Solve: $x - bw = c$ for w

65. Solve: $P = 2L + 2W$ for L

66. Solve: $h = 3(p + 2k)$ for k

67. Solve: $a = \dfrac{x + y + z}{3}$ for y

Section 3.8

68. Solve: $5x \geq -15$

69. Solve: $3x - 4 \leq 8$

70. Solve: $5x > 9x + 4$

71. Solve: $\dfrac{x}{-5} \leq 2$

72. Solve: $4(x - 3) < 3x + 7$

73. Solve: $\dfrac{1}{2}x + 3 \geq \dfrac{2}{3}x - \dfrac{1}{3}$

Answers

Chapter 3 Problems

28. no   29. no   30. yes   31. -14   32. -16   33. 26   34. -2.9   35. -6.4   36. -6

37. 12.5   38. 6   39. 30   40. -7.3   41. 18   42. -12   43. -20   44. 21   45. 10

46. 2   47. 4/9   48. 4.5   49. 3/7   50. -16   51. -122/13   52. -14/11   53. 1

54. 2   55. 14/3   56. -36/7   57. 9   58. -11   59. -36   60. conditional   61. contradiction

62. identity   63. c/a   64. (c - x) / (-b)   65. (P - 2W) / 2   66. (1/6)h - (1/2) p

67. 3a - x - z   68. $x \geq -3$ 69. $x \leq 4$ 70. $x < -1$ 71. $x \geq -10$ 72. $x < 19$ 73. $x \leq 20$

Chapter 4 Test Bank

Multiple Choice

1. Write as a mathematical equation: Four more than a number is sixteen.
   A. $4x = 16$
   B. $x + 4 = 16$
   C. $4 = x + 16$
   D. $4 + 16 = x$

   Answer: B   Section 4.1

2. Write as a mathematical equation: A number is three greater than eleven.
   A. $x + 3 = 11$
   B. $11 = 3 + x$
   C. $x = 11 + 3$
   D. $x = 11 - 3$

   Answer: C   Section 4.1

3. Write as a mathematical equation: A number subtracted from eight is the same as three times the number.
   A. $x - 8 = 3x$
   B. $x - 8 = 3 + x$
   C. $8 - x = 3x$
   D. $8 - x = 3 + x$

   Answer: C   Section 4.1

4. Write as a mathematical equation: If three is added to twice a number, the result equals five less than six times the same number.
   A. $3 + 2x = 5 - 6x$
   B. $3 + 2x = 6x - 5$
   C. $2x - 3 = 6x - 5$
   D. $2x - 3 = 5 - 6x$

   Answer: B   Section 4.1

5. When two thirds of a number is added to three, the sum is fourteen. Find the number.
   A. 16.5
   B. 19.5
   C. 12
   D. 25.4

   Answer: A   Section 4.2

6. The total cost of a mythology book and a poetry book is $78. If the poetry book costs six dollars less than the mythology book, what is the cost of each book?
   A. mythology book: $48   poetry book: $42
   B. mythology book: $46   poetry book: $32
   C. mythology book: $42   poetry book: $36
   D. mythology book: $54   poetry book: $24

   Answer: C   Section 4.2

7. A ten foot rope is cut into two sections. One section is one more than twice the length of the other section. What are the lengths of each section?
   A. One piece is 2 feet and the other piece is 8 feet.
   B. One piece is 3 feet and the other piece is 7 feet.
   C. One piece is 4 feet and the other piece is 6 feet.
   D. One piece is 5 feet and the other piece is 5 feet.

   Answer: B   Section 4.2

8. The plumber charges $50 per service call, then $30 an hour after the first hour. If the bill came to $140, how many hours did the plumber work?
   A. 2 hours
   B. 3 hours
   C. 4 hours
   D. 5 hours

   Answer: C   Section 4.2

9. Find three consecutive even integers such that two thirds of the largest integer is equal to the smallest integer.
   A. 6,8,10
   B. 8,10,12
   C. 10,12,14
   D. 12,14,16

   Answer: B   Section 4.2

10. You earn an 83 and a 91 on your first two German tests. What grade must you earn on the third test to bring your average up to a 90?
    A. 93
    B. 94
    C. 95
    D. 96

    Answer: D   Section 4.2

11. 30% of 240 is what number?
    A. 720
    B. 80
    C. 24
    D. 72

    Answer: D   Section 4.3

12. 44.85 is what percent of 345?
    A. 13%
    B. 15%
    C. 23%
    D. 12%

    Answer: A   Section 4.3

13. A pair of running shoes sold for $78.00 last year. This year, the price has been increased by $4.68. What percent increase is this?
   A. 10%
   B. 9%
   C. 7%
   D. 6%

Answer: D   Section 4.3

14. An antique dealer buys a treasure chest for $2500. If she wants to make a profit of 25%, how much will she mark up the price of the treasure chest?
   A. $25
   B. $250
   C. $625
   D. $540

Answer: C   Section 4.3

15. Carina Marie weighed 8 pounds at birth. At six weeks, she had gained four pounds. What percent increase is this?
   A. 50%
   B. 150%
   C. 25%
   D. 100%

Answer: A   Section 4.3

16. Solve: $\dfrac{x}{14} = \dfrac{10}{35}$
   A. 490
   B. 240
   C. 4
   D. 8

Answer: C   Section 4.4

17. Solve: $\dfrac{1.7}{x} = \dfrac{3.2}{10}$
   A. 5.3125
   B. 0.544
   C. 3.24
   D. 1.435

Answer: A   Section 4.4

18. What is the ratio of 5 centimeters to 1 meter?
   A. $\dfrac{5}{1}$
   B. $\dfrac{1}{5}$
   C. $\dfrac{1}{20}$
   D. $\dfrac{20}{1}$

Answer: C   Section 4.4

19. The tennis team at Fantango Community College won ten of its fifteen matches. Write the ratio of wins to losses.
    A. $\frac{2}{3}$
    B. $\frac{2}{1}$
    C. $\frac{3}{2}$
    D. $\frac{1}{2}$

    Answer: B   Section 4.4

20. Ian can swim one mile in 30 minutes. how many minutes will it take him to swim one third of a mile at this rate?
    A. 10 minutes
    B. 15 minutes
    C. 12 minutes
    D. 20 minutes

    Answer: A   Section 4.4

21. Convert 3 yards to inches.
    A. 15 inches
    B. 12 inches
    C. 108 inches
    D. 36 inches

    Answer: C   Section 4.5

22. Convert 70 kilometers per hour to miles per hour.
    A. 112 miles per hour
    B. 120 miles per hour
    C. 43.75 miles per hour
    D. 14.35 miles per hour

    Answer: C   Section 4.5

23. Change 3 m^2 to ft^2.
    A. 1ft ^{2}
    B. 9ft ^{2}
    C. 32.29 ft^2
    D. 65.4 ft^2

    Answer: C   Section 4.5

24. How many cubic centimeters will a 3.2 liter container hold?
    A. 3.2 cubic centimeters
    B. 32 cubic centimeters
    C. 320 cubic centimeters
    D. 3200 cubic centimeters

    Answer: D   Section 4.5

25. How many square yards of linoleum are needed to cover a kitchen floor which is 18 feet by 10 feet?
    A. 180 square yards
    B. 20 square yards
    C. 90 square yards
    D. 60 square yards

    Answer: B   Section 4.5

Problems

Section 4.1

26. Write as a mathematical equation: Twelve is the same as five and a number.

27. Write as a mathematical equation: Six times an unknown is fifteen.

28. Write as a mathematical equation: The product of a number and sixteen is 102.

29. Write as a mathematical equation: Four less than twice a number is fifteen.

30. Write as a mathematical equation: Twelve minus a number is the same as the number divided by six.

Section 4.2

31. Three times an unknown number is decreased by four and the result is twelve. What is the number?

32. If ten is subtracted from twice a number, the result is the number plus one. Find the number.

33. The sum of two numbers is 76. If one number is one more than twice the other, find both numbers.

34. The perimeter of a rectangular corn field is 320 feet. If the length of the field is three times the width, find the dimensions of the field.

35. Dr. Gulati and Dr. Ampil are both running for head of the surgery ward. The entire hospital staff of 495 votes. Dr. Gulati got 3 less than twice the number of votes Dr. Ampil got. How many votes did each doctor get?

36. Tom's Father is 28 years older than Tom. Two years ago, Tom's Father was twice as old as Tom. How old are Tom and his Father now?

37. Find three consecutive integers whose sum is -72.

38. Find three consecutive odd integers whose sum is 45.

39. Zoe Caldwell, a triathelete, bikes an average of 40 miles per day. If she bikes 35 miles, 70 miles, 20 miles, and 10 miles, how far must she ride on the fifth day to average 40 miles per day?

Section 4.3

40. 15% of what number is 9?

41. Find 120% of 47.

42. Find what percent 53.3 is of 65.

43. 4.7% of what number is 0.094?

44. How much sales tax would you pay on a mountain bike which cost $532.00 if the tax rate is 6.5% ?

45. You got 8 questions wrong out of 72 questions. What percent of the questions did you answer correctly?

46. A bronze alloy contains 65.4% copper. How many kilograms of copper are contained in 200 kilograms of the bronze alloy?

47. The monthly interest rate on Sunshine Charge Card is 1.9% of the unpaid balance. Bobby's unpaid balance is $350. How much interest will he pay this month?

Section 4.4

48. Solve: $\dfrac{4}{w} = \dfrac{12}{15}$

49. Solve: $\dfrac{y}{2} = \dfrac{5}{4}$

50. Solve: $\dfrac{\frac{1}{6}}{\frac{2}{3}} = \dfrac{9}{n}$

51. Solve: $\dfrac{10}{150} = \dfrac{x}{3000}$

52. Find the ratio of one quarter of an hour to two and a half hours.

53. Carina was 21 inches long at birth. When she was six weeks old, she was 2 feet long. What is the ratio of her length at six weeks to her length at birth?

54. A car can travel 253 miles on 10 gallons of gas. How much gas is required to drive 890 miles at this rate?

Section 4.5

55. How many feet are in 3.7 meters?

56. Change 540 square feet to square yards.

57. Convert 60 miles per hour to kilometers per minute.

58. Michelle can run one mile in eight minutes. How fast is her rate in miles per hour?

59. A fish tank is 20 inches by 10 inches by 10 inches. How many gallons of water will fit in the tank?

Answers

Chapter 4 Problems

26. $12 = 5 + x$ 27. $6x = 15$ 28. $16x = 102$ 29. $2x - 4 = 15$ 30. $12 - x = x \div 6$ 31. 16/3

32. 11   33. 25, 51   34. 40 feet by 120 feet   35. Dr. Ampil 166 votes, Dr. Gulati 329 votes

36. Tom: 30, Father: 58   37. -25, -24, -23   38. 13, 15, 17   39. 65 miles   40. 60

41. 56.4   42. 82%   43. 2   44. $34.58   45. 88.89%   46. 130.8 kilograms   47. $6.65

48. 5   49. 2.5   50. 36   51. 200   52. 1/10   53. 8/7   54. 35.18 gallons   55. 12.14 feet

56. 60 yd^2 57. 88 km per min.   58. 7.5 mph   59. 8.66 gallons

Chapter 5 Test Bank

Multiple Choice

1. Simplify: x^4x^6
   A. $x24$
   B. x^{10}
   C. x^2
   D. x^{12}

Answer: B   Section 5.1

2. Simplify: m^7m
   A. m^8
   B. m^6
   C. m^7
   D. m^5

Answer: A   Section 5.1

3. Simplify: $x^2x^3x^5$
   A. $x24$
   B. x^{30}
   C. x^{13}
   D. x^{10}

Answer: D   Section 5.1

4. Simplify: 3^22^4
   A. 144
   B. 48
   C. 58
   D. 40

Answer: A   Section 5.1

5. Simplify: $(5^2)^3$
   A. 5^5
   B. 10^3
   C. 5^6
   D. 5

Answer: C   Section 5.1

6. Simplify: $(ab^2)^4$
   A. ab^8
   B. ab^6
   C. a^4b^8
   D. a^4b^6

Answer: C   Section 5.1

7. Simplify: $(3y)^b$
   A. $3y^b$
   B. 3^by^b
   C. $9y^b$
   D. $3y^b$

Answer: B   Section 5.1

8. Simplify: $\dfrac{w^{12}}{w^{10}}$
    A. w^{22}
    B. w^2
    C. w^5
    D. w^3

9. Simplify: 4^{-7}
    A. -28
    B. -3
    C. -4^7
    D. $\dfrac{1}{4^7}$

10. Simplify: $\dfrac{1}{b^{-5}}$
    A. b^5
    B. $-b^5$
    C. b^4
    D. $-b^4$

11. Simplify: $\dfrac{a^{-5}}{b^7}$
    A. $\dfrac{-a^5}{b^7}$
    B. $\dfrac{1}{a^5b^7}$
    C. $\dfrac{b^7}{a^5}$
    D. $\dfrac{-b^5}{a^7}$

12. Simplify: $5x^{-11}$
    A. $-5x^{11}$
    B. $\dfrac{-5}{x^{11}}$
    C. $\dfrac{5}{x^{11}}$
    D. $5x^{11}$

13. Simplify: 6^0
    A. 1
    B. 0
    C. 6
    D. undefined

14. Simplify: $\left(\frac{3}{4}\right)^{-2}$

    A. $\frac{9}{16}$

    B. $\frac{-9}{16}$

    C. $\frac{16}{9}$

    D. $\frac{16}{-9}$

                                     Answer: C   Section 5.2

15. Simplify: $a^2b^{-2}c^5$

    A. $\frac{a^2c^5}{b^2}$

    B. $\frac{b^2c^5}{a^2}$

    C. $\frac{b^2}{a^2c^5}$

    D. $\frac{a^2b^2}{c^5}$

                                       Answer: A   Section 5.2

16. Simplify: $(-2y^5)^3$

    A. $-6y^8$

    B. $-6y^{15}$

    C. $-8y^8$

    D. $-8y^{15}$

                                       Answer: D   Section 5.3

17. Simplify: $\frac{x^2y^4}{x^7y^3}$

    A. $\frac{y}{x^5}$

    B. $\frac{x^5}{y}$

    C. $\frac{1}{x^5}$

    D. $\frac{y^2}{x^5}$

                                       Answer: A   Section 5.3

18. Simplify: $\dfrac{x^{-3}y^4}{y^{-2}}$

    A. $\dfrac{x^3}{y^2}$

    B. $\dfrac{y^6}{x^3}$

    C. $-\dfrac{y^6}{x^3}$

    D. $\dfrac{y^5}{x}$

Answer: B   Section 5.3

19. Simplify: $\dfrac{x^0 y^{-3}}{x^5 y^6}$

    A. $\dfrac{x^5}{y^9}$

    B. $\dfrac{1}{y^9}$

    C. $\dfrac{1}{x^5 y^9}$

    D. $\dfrac{y^9}{x^5}$

Answer: C   Section 5.3

20. Simplify: $[\,(-6x^{-4})^0\,]^{12}$
    A. 0
    B. 1
    C. -72
    D. -6

Answer: B   Section 5.3

21. Simplify: $\left(\dfrac{3x^{-2}}{y^5}\right)^{-3}$

    A. $\dfrac{-27x^6}{y^{15}}$

    B. $27x^6 y^5$

    C. $27x^6 y^{15}$

    D. $\dfrac{x^6 y^{15}}{27}$

Answer: D   Section 5.3

22. Write in scientific notation: 327,000,000
    A. 32.7×10^7
    B. 3.27×10^8
    C. 32.7×10^{-7}
    D. 3.27×10^{-8}

Answer: B   Section 5.4

23. Write in scientific notation: 0.000059
   A. 59×10^6
   B. 5.9×10^5
   C. 59×10^{-6}
   D. 5.9×10^{-5}

Answer: D   Section 5.4

24. Write in ordinary notation: 3.7×10^{-3}
   A. 3,700
   B. 37,000
   C. 0.00037
   D. 0.0037

Answer: D   Section 5.4

25. Write in ordinary notation: 9.1×10^5
   A. 910,000
   B. 9,100,000
   C. 0.000091
   D. 0.0000091

Answer: A   Section 5.4

26. The moon is approximately 350,000 miles away.
    Write this distance in scientific notation.
   A. 35×10^4
   B. 3.5×10^5
   C. 35×10^{-4}
   D. 3.5×10^{-5}

Answer: B   Section 5.4

27. The rod shaped bacillus bacteria is approximately 2×10^{-7}
    meters in diameter. Write this number in ordinary notation.
   A. 20,000,000
   B. 200,000,000
   C. 0.00000002
   D. 0.0000002

Answer: D   Section 5.4

28. Evaluate using scientific notation: (21,000,000)(3,000)
   A. 7×10^3
   B. 7×10^4
   C. 6.3×10^{10}
   D. 6.3×10^{11}

Answer: C   Section 5.4

29. Evaluate using scientific notation: $\dfrac{140,000}{0.28}$
   A. 5×10^5
   B. 5×10^6
   C. 5×10^{-5}
   D. 5×10^{-6}

Answer: A   Section 5.4

Problems

Section 5.1

30. Simplify: $y^5 y^5$

31. Simplify: $z z^3$

32. Simplify: $3^4 3^2$

33. Simplify: $5^4 5$

34. Simplify: $w^5 w^2 w$

35. Simplify: $(x^2)^7$

36. Simplify: $(3x^3)^2$

37. Simplify: $x^a x^{3a}$

38. Simplify: $\dfrac{y^7}{y^2}$

39. Simplify: $\dfrac{a^7}{a}$

40. Simplify: $\dfrac{z^4}{y}$

41. Simplify: $\left(\dfrac{2x}{y}\right)^3$

42. Simplify: $x^{2a} x^b$

43. Simplify: $(4x)^5$

44. Simplify: $\dfrac{x^3}{x^c}$

Section 5.2

45. Simplify: x^{-10}

46. Simplify: $\dfrac{1}{3^{-2}}$

47. Simplify: $\dfrac{x^{-2}}{y^{-5}}$

48. Simplify: $\dfrac{x^3}{y^{-3}}$

49. Simplify: $\dfrac{1}{xy^{-4}}$

50. Simplify: $\left(\dfrac{a}{b}\right)^{-6}$

51. Simplify: w^0

52. Simplify: $(4ab^2c^7)^0$

53. Simplify: $(-3)^0$

54. Simplify: -9^0

55. Simplify: $\dfrac{9^5}{9^0}$

Section 5.3

56. Simplify: $(3x^4)^2$

57. Simplify: $(4a^5)^{-2}$

58. Simplify: $(9a^2b^0)^2$

59. Simplify: $\dfrac{x^{-5}y^4}{x^{-3}}$

60. Simplify: $\dfrac{x^{-3}y^{-4}}{x^{-1}y^{-7}}$

61. Simplify: $\left(\dfrac{-2x^2}{y^{-3}}\right)^2$

62. Simplify: $(-6x^{-3}y^4)^{-2}$

63. Simplify: $(-27x^{-10})^0$

Section 5.4

64. Write in scientific notation: 2,300

65. Write in scientific notation: 2,070,000

66. Write in scientific notation: 0.013

67. Write in scientific notation: 4.37

124

68. Write in ordinary notation: 4.86×10^{-2}

69. Write in ordinary notation: 7.4×10^{0}

70. Write in ordinary notation: 8.35×10^{3}

71. Mt. Everest is approximately 29,000 feet high. Write this number in scientific notation.

72. The spherical coccus bacteria is aproximately 2×10^{-6} meters in diameter. Write this number in ordinary notation.

73. Evaluate using scientific notation, and express your answer in scientific notation:
    $(0.000014)(0.002)$

74. Evaluate using scientific notation, and express your answer in scientific notation:
    $(5,000,000,000)(0.00043)$

75. Evaluate using scientific notation, and express your answer in scientific notation:
    $$\frac{(0.0015)(35,000,000)}{(0.07)(0.00005)}$$

Answers

Chapter 5 problems

30. y^{10} 31. z^4 32. 3^6 33. 5^5 34. w^8 35. x^{14} 36. $9x^6$ 37. x^{4a}

38. y^5 39. a^6 40. can't simplify   41. $\dfrac{8x^3}{y^3}$ 42. x^{2a+b}

43. 4^5x^5 44. x^{3-c} 45. $\dfrac{1}{x^{10}}$ 46. 9   47. $\dfrac{y^5}{x^2}$ 48. x^3y^3 49. $\dfrac{y^4}{x}$ 50. $\dfrac{b^6}{a^6}$

51. 1   52. 1   53. 1   54. -1   55. 9^5 56. $9x^8$ 57. $\dfrac{1}{16a^{10}}$

58. $81a^4$ 59. $\dfrac{y^4}{x^2}$ 60. $\dfrac{y^3}{x^2}$ 61. $4x^4y^6$ 62. $\dfrac{x^6}{36y^8}$ 63. 1

64. 2.3×10^3 65. 2.07×10^6 66. 1.3×10^{-2} 67. 4.37×10^0 68. 0.0486   69. 7.4

70. 8,350   71. 2.9×10^4 72. 0.000 002   73. 2.8×10^{-8} 74. 2.15×10^6

75. 1.5×10^{10}

Chapter 6 Test Bank

Multiple Choice

1. Write in descending order: $3x^2 - 5 + 7x + 11x^3$
   A. $11x^3 + 7x + 3x^2 - 5$
   B. $-5 + 3x^2 + 7x + 11x^3$
   C. $11x^3 + 3x^2 + 7x - 5$
   D. $-5 + 7x + 3x2 + 11x$

Answer: C   Section 6.1

2. Write in descending order: $4 + 5x^4 - 3x + 11x^2$
   A. $11x^2 + 5x^4 + 4 - 3x$
   B. $5x^4 + 11x^2 - 3x + 4$
   C. $4 - 3x + 11x^2 + 5x^4$
   D. $11x^2 + 4 + 5x^4 - 3x$

Answer: B   Section 6.1

3. What is the degree of: $5x^2 + 7x^3 - 3x + 1$?
   A. 2
   B. 3
   C. 4
   D. 5

Answer: B   Section 6.1

4. What is the degree of: $3x - 2$?
   A. 3
   B. 2
   C. 1
   D. 0

Answer: C   Section 6.1

5. What is the degree of: -4 ?
   A. 4
   B. 2
   C. 1
   D. 0

Answer: D   Section 6.1

6. $4x - 7$ is a :
   A. monomial
   B. binomial
   C. trinomial
   D. none of the above

Answer: B   Section 6.1

7. 13 is a :
   A. monomial
   B. binomial
   C. trinomial
   D. none of the above

Answer: A   Section 6.1

8. $3x^2 - 4x + 7$ is a:
   A. monomial
   B. binomial
   C. trinomial
   D. none of the above

   Answer: C   Section 6.1

9. $7x - 13x^4 + 5x^2 - 11$ is a :
   A. monomial
   B. binomial
   C. trinomial
   D. none of the above

   Answer: D   Section 6.1

10. Add $4x^2 - 3x + 7$ and $-2x^2 + 4x - 11$
    A. $2x^2 + x - 4$
    B. $6x^2 - 7x + 18$
    C. $2x^2 - x - 4$
    D. $6x^2 + 7x - 18$

    Answer: A   Section 6.2

11. Add $3y^2 - 4 + 5y$ and $12y^3 - 3y + 7$
    A. $15y^2 + 12y - 7$
    B. $15y^2 + 2y + 3$
    C. $12y^3 + 3y^2 + 2y + 3$
    D. $12y^3 + 3y^2 - 7y + 12$

    Answer: C   Section 6.2

12. Subtract $5x^2 - 3x + 7$ from $6x^2 + 11x - 5$
    A. $-x^2 - 14x + 12$
    B. $x^2 + 14x - 12$
    C. $11x^2 + 8x + 2$
    D. $11x^2 - 13x + 2$

    Answer: B   Section 6.2

13. Subtract: $(-2y + 3y^2 + 11y^3) - (4y - 5y^3)$
    A. $6y^3 + 3y^2 - 6y$
    B. $6y^3 + 3y^2 + 2y$
    C. $16y^3 + 3y^2 + 6y$
    D. $16y^3 + 3y^2 - 6y$

    Answer: D   Section 6.2

14. Subtract: $(4y^2 - 11y + 10y^3 - 5) - (-3y^4 + 5y^2)$
    A. $-3y^4 + 10y^3 + 9y^2 - 11y - 5$
    B. $3y^4 + 10y^3 - y^2 - 11y - 5$
    C. $-3y^4 - 15y^3 + 9y^2 - 11y - 5$
    D. $3y^4 - 15y^3 - y^2 - 11y - 5$

    Answer: B   Section 6.2

15. Perform the indicated operations:
    $(3x^2 - 5x + 11) - (4x - 5) - (-5x^2 + 7x - 1)$
    A. $-2x^2 + 6x + 5$
    B. $-2x^2 - 6x - 5$
    C. $8x^2 - 16x + 17$
    D. $8x^2 + 9x + 15$

    Answer: C   Section 6.2

16. Multiply: $(3x)(-4x^3)$
    A. $12x^4$
    B. $-12x^4$
    C. $12x^3$
    D. $-12x^3$

Answer: B   Section 6.3

17. Multiply: $(4x^2y)(-2xy^3)(-5xy^7)$
    A. $40x^2y^{10}$
    B. $-40x^2y^{10}$
    C. $40x^4y^{11}$
    D. $-40x^4y^{11}$

Answer: C   Section 6.3

18. Multiply: $-5x(4 - 12x)$
    A. $20x - 60x^2$
    B. $- 20x - 60x^2$
    C. $20x + 60x^2$
    D. $-20x + 60x^2$

Answer: D   Section 6.3

19. Multiply: $-6x^4(5x^3 - 3x + 11)$
    A. $-30x^7 + 18x^5 - 66x^4$
    B. $30x^7 - 18x^5 + 66x^4$
    C. $-30x^{12} + 18x^4 - 11$
    D. $30x^{12} - 18x^5 - 66x^4$

Answer: A   Section 6.3

20. Multiply: $(x - 11)(4x - 3)$
    A. $4x^2 - 47x + 33$
    B. $4x^2 - 15x + 33$
    C. $4x^2 - 15x - 33$
    D. $4x^2 - 47x - 33$

Answer: A   Section 6.3

21. Multiply: $(y + 9)(y^2 + 3y - 10)$
    A. $y^3 - 6y^2 + 17y - 90$
    B. $y^3 - 6y^2 - 37y - 90$
    C. $y^3 + 12y^2 + 17y - 90$
    D. $y^3 - 12y^2 - 17y - 90$

Answer: C   Section 6.3

22. A rectangle has length 2x - 3 and width x + 5.
    Express the area of this rectangle as a polynomial.
    A. $3x + 2$
    B. $2x - 2$
    C. $2x^2 - 2x - 15$
    D. $2x^2 + 7x - 15$

Answer: D   Section 6.3

23. Divide: $(5x^3 - 15x^2 + 20x + 50) \div (-5)$
    A. $-x^3 - 3x^2 + 4x + 10$
    B. $-x^3 + 3x^2 - 4x - 10$
    C. $x^3 + 3x^2 - 4x + 10$
    D. $x^3 - 3x^2 + 4x + 10$

Answer: B   Section 6.4

24. Divide: $(6a^6 - 54a^4 + 36a^2) \div (6a^2)$
   A. $a^3 - 9a^2 + 6a$
   B. $a^3 + 9a^2 - 6a$
   C. $a^4 - 9a^2 + 6$
   D. $a^4 + 9a^2 - 6$

Answer: C   Section 6.4

25. Divide: $(x^2 - 3x + 7) \div (x + 1)$
   A. $x - 4$, remainder 11
   B. $x - 2$, remainder 11
   C. $x - 2$, remainder 5
   D. $x - 4$, remainder 5

Answer: A   Section 6.4

26. Divide: $(3x^2 - 4x + 7) \div (x + 2)$
   A. $3x + 2$, remainder 11
   B. $3x + 2$, remainder 27
   C. $3x - 10$, remainder 11
   D. $3x - 10$, remainder 27

Answer: D   Section 6.4

27. Divide: $(6x^2 - 3x + 7) \div (2x + 1)$
   A. $3x - 3$, remainder 10
   B. $3x$, remainder 7
   C. $3x - 6$, remainder 5
   D. $3x$, remainder 10

Answer: A   Section 6.4

28. Divide: $(5 - 3x^3 + 7x^2) \div (4 - x^2)$
   A. $-3x + 7$, remainder $12x - 33$
   B. $3x - 7$, remainder $-12x + 33$
   C. $-3x + 7$, remainder $-12x + 33$
   D. $3x - 7$, remainder $12x - 33$

Answer: B   Section 6.4

29. The area of a rectangle is $4x^2 - 14x + 6$. Find the width
   if the length is $4x - 2$.
   A. $x + 1$
   B. $2x - 2$
   C. $x - 3$
   D. $2x - 1$

Answer: C   Section 6.4

Problems

Section 6.1

30. Write $3 - 5x^4 + 7x + 11x^2$ in descending order, list the number of terms, the name and the degree of the polynomial.

31. Write $4 - 3x$ in descending order, list the number of terms, the name and the degree of the polynomial.

32. List the number of terms, the name and the degree of the polynomial -20.

33. Write $7x^2 - 2x + 10x^3 - 9x^5 + 20$ in descending order, list the number of terms, the name and the degree of the polynomial.

Section 6.2

34. Add $3 - 2x^2 + 5x^3$ and $7x - 3x^2 + 10$

35. Add $4x^3 - 5x + 7$, $3x + 11x^2 - 5$ and $4 - 5x^2 + 12x$

36. Subtract $3y^3 + 5 - 3y$ from $4y + 5y^3 - 3y^2 + 7$

37. Subtract $4y^4 - 3y^2 + 7$ from $3y - 11$

38. Subtract: $(2x^3 - 5x - 11) - (-3x^2 - 5x + 4)$

39. Perform the indicated operations: $(2x - 11) - (-4x^3 + 7x^2 - 5) + (3x - 12x^2)$

40. Perform the indicated operations: $-(5x^3 - 3x) + (3x^2 - 11) - (-6x + 14)$

Section 6.3

41. Multiply: $(2a^3)(7a^5)$

42. Multiply: $(-6a^2b)(-11a^4b^2)$

43. Multiply: $3x(4x - 1)$

44. Multiply: $4x^3(3x^2 - 5x + 2)$

45. Multiply: $(3x + 1)(x - 4)$

46. Multiply: $(x - 3)(x^2 - 5x + 7)$

47. Multiply: $(4y^3 - 6y + 2)(y - 1)$

48. Multiply: $(5y^2 - 2y + 3)(y^2 + y + 2)$

49. A rectangle has length y - 3 and width 4 - 5y. Express the area of the rectangle as a polynomial.

Section 6.4

50. Divide: $(33x^3 - 27x^2 + 15x) \div (3x)$

51. Divide: $(4b^5 + 8b^4 - 10b^2 + 20b) \div (-4b^2)$

52. Divide: $(44x^5 - 12x^3 + 5x) \div (4x^4)$

53. Divide: $(y^2 + 2y - 3) \div (y - 2)$

54. Divide: $(y^2 + 4y - 21) \div (y + 3)$

55. Divide: $(5 - 3x + x^2) \div (x - 3)$

56. Divide: $(19x - 14 + 3x^2) \div (3x - 2)$

57. Divide: $(x^3 + 5x - 3) \div (x - 1)$

58. Divide: $(b^3 - 8) \div (b - 2)$

59. Divide: $(x^4 - 5x^3 + 3x - 2) \div (x + 3)$

60. Divide: $(x^4 + 3x^2 - 11x + 7) \div (x^2 + 2x - 3)$

61. If the area of a rectangle is $6x^3 - x^2 + 20x + 7$ and the width is 3x + 1, find the length.

Answers

Chapter 6 Problems

30. $5x^4 + 11x^2 + 7x + 3$, 4 terms, polynomial, degree 4   31. $-3x + 4$, 2 terms, binomial ,degree 1

32. 1 term, monomial, degree 0   33. $-9x^5 + 10x^3 + 7x^2 - 2x + 20$, 5 terms, polynomial , degree5

34. $5x^3 - 5x^2 + 7x + 13$ 35. $4x^3 + 6x^2 + 10x + 6$ 36. $2y^3 - 3y^2 + 7y + 2$

37. $-4y^4 + 3y^2 + 3y - 18$ 38. $2x^3 + 3x^2 - 15$ 39. $4x^3 - 19x^2 + 5x - 6$ 40. $-5x^3 + 3x^2 + 9x - 25$

41. $14a^8$ 42. $66a^6b^3$ 43. $12x^2 - 3x$ 44. $12x^5 - 20x^4 + 8x^3$ 45. $3x^2 - 11x - 4$

46. $x^3 - 8x^2 + 22x - 21$ 47. $4y^4 - 4y^3 - 6y^2 + 8y - 2$ 48. $5y^4 + 3y^3 + 11y^2 - y + 6$

49. $19y - 5y^2 - 12$ 50. $11x^2 - 9x + 5$ 51. $-b^3 - 2b^2 + 5/2 - 5/b$ 52. $11x - 3/x + 5/(4x^3)$

53. $y + 4$, rem. 5   54. $y + 1$, rem. -24   55. x, rem. 5   56. $x + 7$ 57. $x^2 + x + 6$, rem. 3

58. $b^2 + 2b + 4$ 59. $x^3 - 8x^2 + 24x - 69$, rem. 205   60. $x^2 - 2x + 10$, rem. $-37x + 37$

61. $2x^2 - x + 7$

Chapter 7 Test Bank

Multiple Choice

1. Factor completely: $5x - 15$
   A. $-10x$
   B. $5(x - 15)$
   C. $5(x - 3)$
   D. prime

   Answer: C   Section 7.1

2. Factor completely: $32x^2 - 40x^5$
   A. $4x^2(8 - 10x^3)$
   B. $8(4x^2 - 5x^5)$
   C. $8x^2(4 - 5x^3)$
   D. prime

   Answer: C   Section 7.1

3. Factor completely: $12x^3y + 24x^2y^4$
   A. $12x^2y(x + 2y^3)$
   B. $12(x^3y + x^2y^3)$
   C. $24(x^3y + x^2y^4)$
   D. prime

   Answer: A   Section 7.1

4. Factor completely: $45x^2y^5 - 50x^3y^3 + 55x^4y^6$
   A. $5(9x^2y^5 - 10x^3y^3 + 11x^4y^6)$
   B. $5x^2y^3(9y^2 - 10x + 11x^2y^3)$
   C. $5x^2y^3(9y^2 - 10y + 55x^2y^3)$
   D. prime

   Answer: B   Section 7.1

5. Factor completely: $3x + 4y - 7z$
   A. $x(3 + 4y - 7z)$
   B. $3(x + 4y - 7z)$
   C. $y(3x + 4 - 7z)$
   D. prime

   Answer: D   Section 7.1

6. Multiply: $(x + 2)(x + 3)$
   A. $x^2 + 5x + 5$
   B. $x^2 + x + 6$
   C. $x^2 + x + 5$
   D. $x^2 + 5x + 6$

   Answer: D   Section 7.2

7. Multiply: $(x - 10)(x - 4)$
   A. $x^2 - 10x + 14$
   B. $x^2 + 14x - 40$
   C. $x^2 - 14x + 40$
   D. $x^2 + 14x + 40$

   Answer: C   Section 7.2

8. Multiply: $(2x + 3)(x - 1)$
   A. $2x^2 - 6x - 3$
   B. $2x^2 + x - 3$
   C. $2x^2 + 6x - 3$
   D. $2x^2 - x - 3$

   Answer: B   Section 7.2

9. Multiply: $(5x - 3)(5x + 3)$
   A. $25x^2 - 9$
   B. $25x^2 - 30x - 9$
   C. $25x^2 + 30x - 9$
   D. $25x^2 + 9$

   Answer: A   Section 7.2

10. Multiply: $(x + 4)^2$
    A. $x^2 + 16$
    B. $x^2 + 8$
    C. $x^2 + 8x + 16$
    D. $x^2 + 16x + 16$

   Answer: C   Section 7.2

11. Factor completely: $x^2 + 3x - 4$
    A. $(x - 4)(x + 1)$
    B. $(x - 4)(x - 1)$
    C. $(x + 4)(x - 1)$
    D. prime

   Answer: C   Section 7.3

12. Factor completely: $x^2 - x - 12$
    A. $(x - 4)(x + 3)$
    B. $(x - 4)(x - 3)$
    C. $(x + 4)(x + 3)$
    D. prime

   Answer: A   Section 7.3

13. Factor completely: $x^2 - 8x + 7$
    A. $(x + 7)(x + 1)$
    B. $(x- 7)(x - 1)$
    C. $(x + 7(x - 1)$
    D. prime

   Answer: B   Section 7.3

14. Factor completely: $x^2 - 12x + 27$
    A. $(x - 10)(x - 2)$
    B. $(x - 9)(x - 3)$
    C. $(x - 9)(x + 3)$
    D. prime

   Answer: B   Section 7.3

15. Factor completely: $x^2 + x + 1$
    A. $(x - 1)(x - 1)$
    B. $(x + 1)(x + 1)$
    C. $(x - 1)(x + 1)$
    D. prime

   Answer: D   Section 7.3

16. Factor completely: $3x^2 - 8x - 3$
   A. $(x + 3)(3x + 1)$
   B. $(x - 3)(3x + 1)$
   C. $(x + 3)(3x - 1)$
   D. prime

Answer: B   Section 7.4

17. Factor completely: $2x^2 - 11x + 12$
   A. $(x - 4)(2x - 3)$
   B. $(x - 3)(2x - 4)$
   C. $(x + 4)(2x + 3)$
   D. prime

Answer: A   Section 7.4

18. Factor completely: $5x^2 - x + 1$
   A. $(5x - 1)(x + 1)$
   B. $(5x + 1)(x + 1)$
   C. $(5x - 1)(x - 1)$
   D. prime

Answer: D   Section 7.4

19. Factor completely: $14a^2 + a - 3$
   A. $(7a - 3)(2a + 1)$
   B. $(7a + 3)(2a - 1)$
   C. $(7a - 1)(2a + 3)$
   D. prime

Answer: A   Section 7.4

20. Factor completely: $48x^2 + 113x - 40$
   A. $(16x + 5)(3x - 8)$
   B. $(8x - 5)(6x + 8)$
   C. $(3x + 8)(16x - 5)$
   D. prime

Answer: C   Section 7.4

21. Factor completely: $a^2 - 81$
   A. $(a + 27)(a - 3)$
   B. $(a - 27)(a + 3)$
   C. $(a - 9)(a + 9)$
   D. prime

Answer: C   Section 7.5

22. Factor completely: $4a^2 - 1$
   A. $(4a - 1)(a + 1)$
   B. $(2a - 1)(2a + 1)$
   C. $(2a - 1)(2a - 1)$
   D. prime

Answer: B   Section 7.5

23. Factor completely: $25x^2 - 16y^2$
   A. $(5x - 4y)(5x + 4y)$
   B. $(5x - 4y)(5x - 4y)$
   C. $(5x + 4y)(5x + 4y)$
   D. prime

Answer: A   Section 7.5

24. Factor completely: $y^2 + 100$
   A. $(y + 10)(y - 10)$
   B. $(y - 10)(y - 10)$
   C. $(y + 10)(y + 10)$
   D. prime

25. Factor completely: $144a^2b^4 - 25c^6$
   A. $(12a^2b^2 - 5c^6)(12a^2b^2 + 5c^6)$
   B. $(12ab^4 - 5c^3)(12ab^4 + 5c^3)$
   C. $(12ab^2 - 5c^3)(12ab^2 + 5c^3)$
   D. prime

26. Factor completely: $5a^2 - 5b^2$
   A. $(5a - b)(5a + b)$
   B. $5(a + b)(a - b)$
   C. $(5a - b)(a - 5b)$
   D. prime

27. Factor completely: $4x^2 + 4x - 24$
   A. $(4x - 8)(x + 3)$
   B. $(x - 2)(4x + 12)$
   C. $4(x - 2)(x + 3)$
   D. prime

28. Factor completely: $3a^3 + 6a^2b + 3ab^2$
   A. $3a(a + b)(a + b)$
   B. $(3a^2 + ab)(a + b)$
   C. $(a + b)(3a^2 + 3ab)$
   D. prime

29. Factor completely: $5x^3 + 5x^2 - 10x$
   A. $5x(x^2 + x - 2)$
   B. $5x(x - 2)(x + 1)$
   C. $5x(x + 2)(x - 1)$
   D. prime

30. Factor completely: $12w^2 + 7wz + z^2$
   A. $(3w - z)(4w + z)$
   B. $(3w + z)(4w + z)$
   C. $(3w - z)(4w - z)$
   D. prime

Problems

Section 7.1

31. Factor completely: $7 + 21x$

32. Factor completely: $26x^3 - 39x^2$

33. Factor completely: $14a^2 - 21b$

34. Factor completely: $6a^2b - 4ab^2$

35. Factor completely: $4w - 5z$

36. Factor completely: $-3w^2 - 5wy + 4wy^2$

37. Factor completely: $12a^2b^3c^4 + 21ab^2c^5$

38. Factor completely: $-12x^2 - 3xy + 5y^3$

Section 7.2

39. Multiply: $(x - 3)(x + 7)$

40. Multiply: $(x - 7)(x - 5)$

41. Multiply: $(x - 4)(3x + 2)$

42. Multiply: $(4x + 1)(3x - 2)$

43. Multiply: $(4a - b)(4a + b)$

44. Multiply: $(a - 3)^2$

45. Multiply: $(2x - 3)^2$

46. Multiply: $(3y + 5)^2$

Section 7.3

47. Factor completely: $x^2 - 5x - 6$

48. Factor completely: $x^2 + 6x - 27$

49. Factor completely: $x^2 + 3x + 2$

50. Factor completely: $x^2 - 3x + 4$

51. Factor completely: $x^2 + 101x + 100$

52. Factor completely: $x^2 + 5x - 45$

53. Factor completely: $x^2 + 9x - 10$

54. Factor completely: $x^2 + 4x - 12$

55. Factor completely: $x^2 + x - 6$

Section 7.4

56. Factor completely: $2x^2 + 7x + 3$

57. Factor completely: $4x^2 - 5x - 6$

58. Factor completely: $6x^2 - 5x - 4$

59. Factor completely: $10x^2 - 11x + 3$

60. Factor completely: $3x^2 - 6x + 7$

61. Factor completely: $40a^2 - 2a - 21$

Section 7.5

62. Factor completely: $x^2 - 25$

63. Factor completely: $b^2 - 100$

64. Factor completely: $16x^2 - 25$

65. Factor completely: $x^2 + 9$

66. Factor completely: $64a^2 + b^2$

67. Factor completely: $x^4 - 81$

68. Factor completely: $y^8 - 25$

69. Factor completely: $100x^{10} - 49x^6z^8$

Section 7.6

70. Factor completely: $44x^2 - 11y^2$

71. Factor completely: $6a^4 - 36b^2$

72. Factor completely: $14a^2 - 49a - 28$

73. Factor completely: $-3x^2 - 25x - 28$

74. Factor completely: $4x^3y^2 + 8x^2y^2 - 12xy^2$

75. Factor completely: $x^2 - xy - 6y^2$

76. Factor completely: $2a^2 + 7ab - 15b^2$

77. Factor completely: $5x^2 - 10x - 15$

78. Factor completely: $25x^2y - 100y^3$

Answers

Chapter 7 Problems

31. $7(1 + 3x)$ 32. $13x^2(2x - 3)$ 33. $7(2a^2 - 3b)$ 34. $2b(3a - 2ab)$ 35. prime

36. $w(-3w - 5y + 4y^2)$ 37. $3ab^2c^4(4ab + 7c)$ 38. prime   39. $x^2 + 4x - 21$

40. $x^2 - 12x + 35$ 41. $3x^2 - 10x - 8$ 42. $12x^2 - 5x - 2$ 43. $16a^2 - b^2$ 44. $a^2 - 6a + 9$

45. $4x^2 - 12x + 9$ 46. $9y^2 + 30y + 25$ 47. $(x - 6)(x + 1)$ 48. $(x - 3)(x + 9)$

49. $(x + 2)(x + 1)$ 50. prime   51. $(x + 100)(x + 1)$ 52. prime   53. $(x - 1)(x + 10)$

54. $(x - 2)(x + 6)$ 55. $(x - 2)(x + 3)$ 56. $(2x + 1)(x + 3)$ 57. $(x - 2)(4x + 3)$

58. $(2x + 1)(3x - 4)$ 59. $(5x - 3)(2x - 1)$ 60. prime   61. $(10a + 7)(4a - 3)$

62. $(x - 5)(x + 5)$ 63. $(b - 10)(b + 10)$ 64. $(4x - 5)(4x + 5)$ 65. prime   66. prime

67. $(x - 3)(x + 3)(x^2 + 9)$ 68. $(y^4 - 5)(y^4 + 5)$ 69. $(10x^5 - 7x^3z^4)(10x^5 + 7x^3z^4)$

70. $11(2x - y)(2x + y)$ 71. $6(a^4 - 6b^2)$ 72. $7(2a + 1)(a - 4)$ 73. $(-3x - 4)(x + 7)$

74. $4xy^2(x - 1)(x + 3)$ 75. $(x - 3y)(x + 2y)$ 76. $(2a - 3b)(a + 5b)$ 77. $5(x - 3)(x + 1)$

78. $25y(x - 2y)(x + 2y)$

Chapter 8 Test Bank

Multiple Choice

1. Find the value(s) of the variable (if any) for which the fraction $\dfrac{4}{x-3}$ is undefined.
   A. $x = -3$
   B. $x = 3$
   C. $x = 0$
   D. no value

   Answer: B   Section 8.1

2. Find the value(s) of the variable (if any) for which the fraction $\dfrac{3}{x^2-1}$ is undefined.
   A. $x = 1$
   B. $x = -1$
   C. $x = 1$ and $x = -1$
   D. no value

   Answer: C   Section 8.1

3. Find the value(s) of the variable (if any) for which the fraction $\dfrac{9}{x^2+16}$ is undefined.
   A. $x = 4$
   B. $x = -4$
   C. $x = 4$ and $x = -4$
   D. no value

   Answer: D   Section 8.1

4. Find the missing term: $\dfrac{4}{3} = \dfrac{?}{-3}$
   A. 4
   B. -4
   C. 12
   D. -12

   Answer: B   Section 8.1

5. Find the missing term: $\dfrac{1-y}{2-x} = \dfrac{y-1}{?}$
   A. $x - 2$
   B. $x + 2$
   C. $2 - x$
   D. $-2 - x$

   Answer: A   Section 8.1

6. Reduce to lowest terms, if possible: $\dfrac{36x^2y^3}{18xy^5}$

   A. $\dfrac{2x}{y^3}$

   B. $2xy^2$

   C. $\dfrac{2x}{y^2}$

   D. can't reduce

                                                Answer: C   Section 8.2

7. Reduce to lowest terms, if possible: $\dfrac{-27x^2y^2z^5}{-3xy^3z^2}$

   A. $\dfrac{9xz^3}{y}$

   B. $9xyz^3$

   C. $\dfrac{9x}{yz^3}$

   D. can't reduce

                                                Answer: A   Section 8.2

8. Reduce to lowest terms, if possible: $\dfrac{5}{15x - 20}$

   A. $\dfrac{1}{3x - 20}$

   B. $\dfrac{1}{15x - 4}$

   C. $\dfrac{1}{3x - 4}$

   D. can't reduce

                                                Answer: C   Section 8.2

9. Reduce to lowest terms, if possible: $\dfrac{x^2 - 5x + 6}{3x^2 - 27}$

   A. $\dfrac{x - 2}{3(x + 3)}$

   B. $\dfrac{x - 2}{3(x + 3)}$

   C. $\dfrac{3(x - 2)}{x - 3}$

   D. can't reduce

                                                Answer: B   Section 8.2

10. Reduce to lowest terms, if possible: $\dfrac{9-x}{x^2-9}$

    A. $\dfrac{1}{x+3}$

    B. $\dfrac{-1}{x+3}$

    C. $\dfrac{1}{x-3}$

    D. can't reduce

                                      Answer: D   Section 8.2

11. Perform the indicated operation and reduce: $\dfrac{14x^2}{5y} \cdot \dfrac{25y^3}{21x}$

    A. $\dfrac{10xy^2}{3}$

    B. $\dfrac{10x^2y^3}{3}$

    C. $\dfrac{10x^2}{3y^2}$

    D. $\dfrac{10y^3}{3x}$

                                        Answer: A   Section 8.3

12. Perform the indicated operation and reduce: $\dfrac{2a^3-2ab^2}{ab^2} \div \dfrac{16a+16b}{4a^3}$

    A. $\dfrac{(a+b)a^3}{2b^2}$

    B. $\dfrac{(a-b)a^3}{8b^2}$

    C. $\dfrac{(a-b)a^3}{2b^2}$

    D. $\dfrac{(a-1)a^2}{2b}$

                                        Answer: C   Section 8.3

13. Perform the indicated operation and reduce: $\dfrac{5x - 3}{x^2 + 3x + 4} \div \dfrac{25x - 15}{x + 1}$

A. $\dfrac{x + 1}{5(x^2 + 3x + 4)}$

B. $\dfrac{1}{5(x^2 + 3x + 4)}$

C. $\dfrac{1}{5(x + 4)}$

D. $\dfrac{1}{5(x - 4)}$

Answer: A   Section 8.3

14. Perform the indicated operation and reduce: $\dfrac{x^2 - 25}{5x - 15} \cdot \dfrac{x^2 - 9}{x^2 + 25}$

A. $\dfrac{(x - 5)(x + 3)}{5(x + 5)}$

B. $\dfrac{(x - 5)(x + 5)}{5(x - 3)}$

C. $\dfrac{(x - 5)(x + 5)(x - 3)}{5(x + 5)}$

D. $\dfrac{(x - 5)(x + 5)(x + 3)}{5(x^2 + 25)}$

Answer: D   Section 8.3

15. Perform the indicated operation and reduce: $\dfrac{b - a}{a^3 - ab^2} \cdot \dfrac{a^2 b}{a^2 + b^2}$

A. $\dfrac{b - a}{(a^2 - b^2)(a^2 + b^2)}$

B. $\dfrac{-ab}{(a + b)(a^2 + b^2)}$

C. $\dfrac{-1}{(a^2 + b^2)}$

D. $\dfrac{-ab}{(a + b)^3}$

Answer: B   Section 8.3

16. Perform the indicated operations and reduce to lowest terms: $\dfrac{7a}{5} - \dfrac{2a}{5}$

A. $5a$
B. a
C. a^2
D. $5a^2$

Answer: B   Section 8.4

17. Perform the indicated operations and reduce to lowest terms: $\dfrac{6a}{2a - b} - \dfrac{3b}{2a - b}$

A. $\dfrac{6a - 3b}{2a - b}$
B. $\dfrac{6a + 3b}{2a - b}$
C. $\dfrac{3a - 3b}{a - b}$
D. 3

Answer: D   Section 8.4

18. Perform the indicated operations and reduce to lowest terms: $\dfrac{3b}{b^2 - 25} + \dfrac{15}{b^2 - 25}$

A. $\dfrac{3}{b - 5}$
B. $\dfrac{3b + 15}{(b + 5)(b - 5)}$
C. $\dfrac{3b + 3}{b - 5}$
D. $\dfrac{3}{b + 5}$

Answer: A   Section 8.4

19. Find the LCD for the fractions: $\dfrac{4}{x^2y} , \dfrac{3a}{xy^3}$

A. x^2y
B. xy^3
C. x^3y^4
D. x^2y^3

Answer: D   Section 8.4

20. Find the LCD for the fractions: $\dfrac{4}{x^2 - 1} , \dfrac{3x}{x + 1}$

A. $(x^2 - 1)(x + 1)$
B. $(x + 1)(x - 1)$
C. $(x + 1)^2$
D. $(x - 1)^2$

Answer: B   Section 8.4

21. Find the missing numerator: $\dfrac{3}{7x^2y} = \dfrac{?}{21x^3y^4}$

    A. $9xy^3$
    B. $21xy^3$
    C. $9x^3y^4$
    D. $21x^3y^4$

Answer: A   Section 8.4

22. Find the missing numerator: $\dfrac{3}{x+2} = \dfrac{?}{3x(x+2)}$

    A. $3x$
    B. $9x$
    C. $3x^2$
    D. $9x^2$

Answer: B   Section 8.4

23. Perform the indicated operation and reduce: $\dfrac{4}{3x^2} + \dfrac{5}{2x}$

    A. $\dfrac{9}{3x^2 + 2x}$

    B. $\dfrac{20}{3x^2 + 2x}$

    C. $\dfrac{8 + 15x}{6x^2}$

    D. $\dfrac{4 + 5x}{x^2}$

Answer: C   Section 8.5

24. Perform the indicated operation and reduce: $3 - \dfrac{5}{2x}$

    A. $\dfrac{6x - 5}{2x}$

    B. $\dfrac{3x - 5}{2x}$

    C. $\dfrac{-2}{x}$

    D. -2

Answer: A   Section 8.5

25. Perform the indicated operation and reduce: $\dfrac{7}{x^2 - 9} + \dfrac{2}{x + 3}$

    A. $\dfrac{2x + 13}{(x + 3)(x - 3)}$

    B. $\dfrac{2x + 1}{(x - 3)(x + 3)}$

    C. $\dfrac{9}{x^2 + x - 6}$

    D. $\dfrac{5}{x^2 + x - 6}$

                                            Answer: B   Section 8.5

26. Perform the indicated operation and reduce: $\dfrac{3}{x^2 - 5x + 6} + \dfrac{2}{x^2 - 4}$

    A. $\dfrac{5}{2x^2 - 5x + 2}$

    B. $\dfrac{6}{2x^2 - 5x + 2}$

    C. $\dfrac{x}{(x - 3)(x - 2)(x + 2)}$

    D. $\dfrac{5x}{(x - 3)(x - 2)(x + 2)}$

                                            Answer: D   Section 8.5

27. Perform the indicated operation and reduce: $\dfrac{3x + 1}{5x} + \dfrac{2x + 1}{3x}$

    A. $\dfrac{5x + 2}{8x}$

    B. $\dfrac{x}{8x}$

    C. $\dfrac{19x + 8}{15x}$

    D. $\dfrac{-x - 2}{15x}$

                                            Answer: C   Section 8.5

28. Simplify: $\dfrac{\frac{x}{y^3}}{\frac{x^4}{y^2}}$

A. $\dfrac{xy^2}{y^3x^4}$

B. $\dfrac{y}{x^3}$

C. $\dfrac{1}{yx^3}$

D. $\dfrac{x^3}{y}$

Answer: C   Section 8.6

29. Simplify: $\dfrac{\frac{1}{2x} - \frac{1}{x}}{\frac{3}{5x}}$

A. $\dfrac{5x}{3}$

B. $\dfrac{-5}{6}$

C. $\dfrac{5}{6}$

D. $\dfrac{-x}{5}$

Answer: B   Section 8.6

30. Simplify: $\dfrac{\frac{1}{a} - \frac{1}{b}}{a - b}$

A. $\dfrac{a + b}{-ab}$

B. $\dfrac{a - b}{ab}$

C. $\dfrac{b - a}{ab(a - b)}$

D. $\dfrac{-1}{ab}$

Answer: D   Section 8.6

31. Simplify: $\dfrac{1 - \dfrac{2}{x} + \dfrac{3}{x^2}}{\dfrac{9}{x} - x}$

    A. $\dfrac{x^2 - 2x + 3}{9x - x^3}$

    B. $\dfrac{x^2 - 2x + 3}{9 - x^2}$

    C. $\dfrac{x + 1}{-x(x + 3)}$

    D. $\dfrac{x - 1}{9x - x^3}$

Answer: A   Section 8.6

32. Solve and check: $\dfrac{4}{x - 3} = \dfrac{5}{x + 1}$

    A. $x = 7$
    B. $x = 3$
    C. $x = 19$
    D. no solution

Answer: C   Section 8.7

33. Solve and check: $\dfrac{3}{x} - \dfrac{1}{3x} = \dfrac{1}{5}$

    A. $x = 40/3$
    B. $x = 10$
    C. $x = 8$
    D. no solution

Answer: A   Section 8.7

34. Solve and check: $\dfrac{1}{5x} + \dfrac{2}{3} = \dfrac{1}{5x}$

    A. $x = 0$
    B. $x = 5$
    C. $x = 3$
    D. no solution

Answer: D   Section 8.7

35. Solve and check: $\dfrac{2a + 1}{a^2 - 4} - \dfrac{3}{a + 2} = \dfrac{-4}{a - 2}$

    A. $a = -1$
    B. $a = -2$
    C. $a = -3$
    D. no solution

Answer: A   Section 8.7

36. The reciprocal of a number plus one half is the same as two thirds. Find the numbers.
   A. $x = 3$
   B. $x = 6$
   C. $x = -3$
   D. no solution

Answer: B   Section8.7

Problems

36. Find the value(s) of the variable (if any) for which the fraction $\dfrac{5x + 1}{3x - 2}$ is undefined.

37. Find the value(s) of the variable (if any) for which the fraction $\dfrac{7}{-4x}$ is undefined.

38. Find the value(s) of the variable (if any) for which the fraction $\dfrac{4x - 3}{x^2 - 2x + 1}$ is undefined.

39. Find the value(s) of the variable (if any) for which the fraction $\dfrac{3x}{x^3 + 7x^2 - 30x}$ is undefined.

40. Find the missing term: $\dfrac{2}{-x} = \dfrac{-2}{?}$

41. Find the missing term: $\dfrac{4}{x - 3} = \dfrac{?}{3 - x}$

42. Find the missing term: $\dfrac{-3}{x - 2} = \dfrac{?}{-(x - 2)}$

Section 8.2

43. Reduce to lowest terms, if possible: $\dfrac{-6x^4y}{24x^3y}$

44. Reduce to lowest terms, if possible: $\dfrac{14a^3b^2}{24cd^4}$

45. Reduce to lowest terms, if possible: $\dfrac{4x^2 - 4}{x + 2}$

46. Reduce to lowest terms, if possible: $\dfrac{x - 5}{x + 5}$

47. Reduce to lowest terms, if possible: $\dfrac{x^3 - 25x}{5x^2 + 25x}$

48. Reduce to lowest terms, if possible: $\dfrac{x^2 - 16}{4 - x}$

49. Reduce to lowest terms, if possible: $\dfrac{x^2 + 100}{10 + x}$

50. Perform the indicated operation: $\dfrac{23a^2b^4}{15c^5} \div \dfrac{46a^5b}{30c}$

51. Perform the indicated operation: $\dfrac{2a^3 - 2ab^2}{ab^2} \div \dfrac{16a + 16b}{4a^3}$

52. Perform the indicated operation: $\dfrac{x - y}{4x^2} \bullet \dfrac{36x^4}{x^2 - y^2}$

53. Perform the indicated operation: $\dfrac{x^2 - 3x + 2}{x^2 - 1} \bullet \dfrac{x^2 + x}{4x - 8}$

54. Perform the indicated operation: $\dfrac{(x + 2)^2}{x^2 - 4} \bullet \dfrac{5x - 10}{x^2 - 9}$

55. Perform the indicated operation: $\dfrac{3x^2 + 6x + 3}{3x - 2} \div \dfrac{6x - 9}{21x - 14}$

Section 8.4

56. Perform the indicated operation and reduce to lowest terms: $\dfrac{-2}{3x} - \dfrac{4}{3x}$

57. Perform the indicated operation and reduce to lowest terms: $\dfrac{5}{b - 1} - \dfrac{5b}{b - 1}$

58. Perform the indicated operation and reduce to lowest terms: $\dfrac{x - 3}{3x^2 - 6x} + \dfrac{x + 2}{3x^2 - 6x} - \dfrac{4x - 3}{3x^2 - 6x}$

59. Find the LCD for the fractions: $\dfrac{2}{x - 3}, \dfrac{5}{x}$

60. Find the LCD for the fractions: $\dfrac{3}{x^2 - 5x + 6}, \dfrac{7}{x^3 - 9x}$

61. Find the LCD for the fractions: $\dfrac{10}{6x^3y^2z}, \dfrac{3}{5xy^4z^2}, \dfrac{2}{15x^3yz}$

62. Find the missing numerator: $\dfrac{4}{5ab^3} = \dfrac{?}{25a^2b^5}$

63. Find the missing numerator: $\dfrac{5x}{x - 5} = \dfrac{?}{(x + 1)(x - 5)}$

64. Find the missing numerator: $\dfrac{x - 1}{(x + 5)(x - 4)} = \dfrac{?}{(x + 5)(x - 3)(x - 4)}$

Section 8.5

65. Perform the indicated operation and reduce: $\dfrac{5}{x} - \dfrac{3}{x^3}$

66. Perform the indicated operation and reduce: $\dfrac{5}{ab^2c} - \dfrac{2a}{a^2bc^3}$

67. Perform the indicated operation and reduce: $\dfrac{4x}{x-3} + \dfrac{-12}{x+1}$

68. Perform the indicated operation and reduce: $\dfrac{4}{x} - \dfrac{5}{x-2}$

69. Perform the indicated operation and reduce: $\dfrac{2x}{1-x} - \dfrac{2}{x-1}$

70. Perform the indicated operation and reduce: $\dfrac{5}{x^2+1} + \dfrac{2}{x-1}$

Section 8.6

71. Simplify: $\dfrac{\frac{3}{2a}}{4b}$

72. Simplify: $\dfrac{\frac{x}{2} - \frac{1}{x}}{1 - \frac{3}{x}}$

73. Simplify: $\dfrac{\frac{4a^2}{3b}}{\frac{5a^4}{b^2}}$

74. Simplify: $\dfrac{\frac{x-3}{y}}{\frac{x^2-9}{2y}}$

75. Simplify: $\dfrac{\frac{4}{x-1} + \frac{1}{x}}{\frac{1}{x} - \frac{3}{x-1}}$

76. Simplify: $\dfrac{5b}{1 + \frac{b+1}{b-1}}$

77. Solve and check: $\dfrac{2x}{3x-2} = \dfrac{5}{4}$

78. Solve and check: $\dfrac{x}{2} - \dfrac{3x}{5} = \dfrac{1}{6}$

79. Solve and check: $\dfrac{2}{x-3} + \dfrac{4}{x+3} = \dfrac{1}{x^2-9}$

80. Solve and check: $\dfrac{2x}{x+1} - \dfrac{4}{x+1} = 1$

81. Solve and check: $\dfrac{5}{x+1} + \dfrac{3}{x-1} = \dfrac{6}{x^2-1}$

82. Solve and check: $\dfrac{1}{b-1} + 1 = \dfrac{b-1}{b}$

83. Four divided by the quantity of a number plus four is the same as negative two over three times the number.

Answers

Chapter 8 Problems

36. $x = \dfrac{2}{3}$ 37. $x = 0$ 38. $x = 1$ 39. $x = 0, 3, -10$ 40. x 41. -4 42. 3

43. $\dfrac{-x}{4}$ 44. $\dfrac{7a^3b^2}{12cd^4}$ 45. can't reduce   46. can't reduce   47. $\dfrac{x-5}{5}$

48. $-(x+4)$ 49. can't reduce   50. $\dfrac{b^3}{c^4a^3}$ 51. $\dfrac{a^3(a-b)}{2b^2}$ 52. $\dfrac{9x^2}{x+y}$

53. $\dfrac{x}{4}$ 54. $\dfrac{5(x+2)}{x^2-9}$ 55. $\dfrac{7(x^2+2x+1)}{2x-3}$ 56. $\dfrac{-2}{x}$ 57. -5

58. $\dfrac{-2x+2}{3x(x-2)}$ 59. $x(x-3)$ 60. $x(x-3)(x+3)(x-2)$ 61. $30x^3y^4z^2$ 62. $20ab^2$ 63. $5x(x+1)$

64. $(x-1)(x-3)$ 65. $\dfrac{5x^2-3}{x^3}$ 66. $\dfrac{5ac^2-2ab}{a^2b^2c^3}$ 67. $\dfrac{4x^2-8x+36}{(x-3)(x+1)}$

68. $\dfrac{-x-8}{x(x-2)}$ 69. $\dfrac{2x+2}{1-x}$ 70. $\dfrac{2x^2+5x-3}{(x^2+1)(x-1)}$ 71. $\dfrac{3}{8ab}$ 72. $\dfrac{x^2-2}{2x-6}$

73. $\dfrac{4b}{15a^2}$ 74. $\dfrac{2}{x+3}$ 75. $\dfrac{5x-1}{-2x-1}$ 76. $\dfrac{5(b-1)}{2}$ 77. $\dfrac{10}{7}$

78. $\dfrac{-5}{3}$ 79. $\dfrac{7}{6}$ 80. 5 81. no solution   82. $\dfrac{1}{2}$ 83. $\dfrac{-4}{7}$

Chapter 9 Test Bank

Multiple Choice

1. Which quadrant is (-2, 3) located in?
   A. Quadrant I
   B. Quadrant II
   C. Quadrant III
   D. Quadrant IV

   Answer: B   Section 9.1

2. Which quadrant is (4, 0.5) located in?
   A. Quadrant I
   B. Quadrant II
   C. Quadrant III
   D. Quadrant IV

   Answer: A   Section 9.1

3. Which quadrant is (6, -3) located in?
   A. Quadrant I
   B. Quadrant II
   C. Quadrant III
   D. Quadrant IV

   Answer: D   Section 9.1

4. Which quadrant is (-1, -5) located in?
   A. Quadrant I
   B. Quadrant II
   C. Quadrant III
   D. Quadrant IV

   Answer: C   Section 9.1

5. Which quadrant is (4, 0) located in?
   A. no Quadrant
   B. Quadrant II and III
   C. Quadrant III and IV
   D. Quadrant IV and I

   Answer: A   Section 9.1

6. The graph of x - y = 4 looks like:

A.

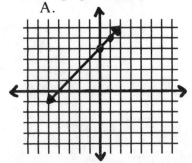

B.

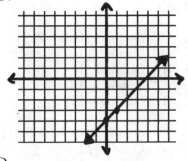

C.

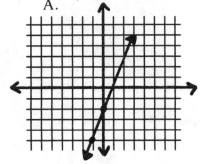

D.

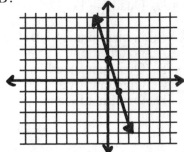

Answer: B   Sections 9.2&9.4

7. The graph of 3x + y = -2 looks like:

A.

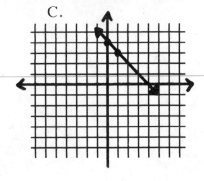

B.

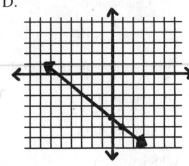

C.

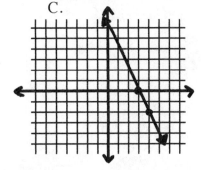

D.

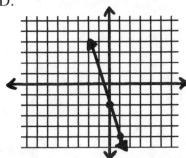

Answer: D   Sections 9.2&9.4

8. The graph of $2x + 5y = 10$ looks like:

A.

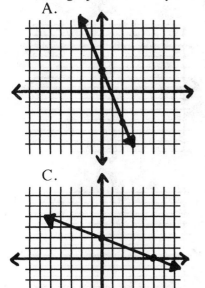

B.

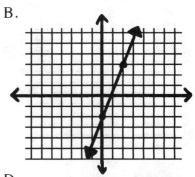

C.

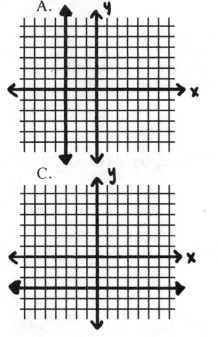

D.

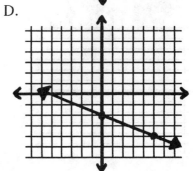

Answer: C   Sections 9.2&9.4

9. The graph of $x = -3$ looks like:

A.

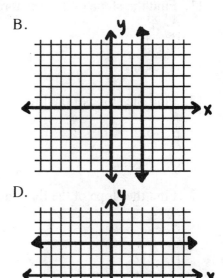

B.

C.

D.

Answer: A   Sections 9.2&9.4

10. The graph of y = 4 looks like:

A.

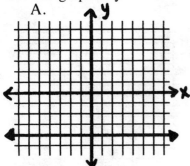

B.

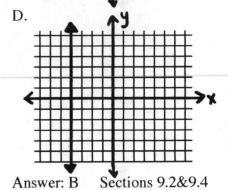

C.

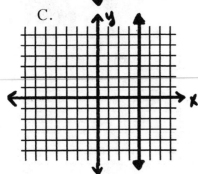

D.

Answer: B   Sections 9.2&9.4

11. Find the slope of the line through the points: (4,2), (5,6)
   A. 4
   B. -4
   C. 8/9
   D. -8/9

Answer: A   Section 9.3

12. Find the slope of the line through the points: (5, -1), (-3, 4)
   A. 3/2
   B. -3/2
   C. 5/8
   D. -5/8

Answer: D   Section 9.3

13. Find the slope of the line through the points: (-3, -2), (-5, -1)
   A. 2
   B. -2
   C. 1/2
   D. -1/2

Answer: D   Section 9.3

14. Find the slope of the line through the points: (5,0), (-2,0)
   A. 3
   B. 7
   C. 0
   D. undefined

Answer: C   Section 9.3

160

15. Find the slope and the y-intercept of the line having the given equation: $y = 3x - 5$
    A. $m = -5$, y-intercept = 3
    B. $m = 5$, y-intercept = -3
    C. $m = 3$, y-intercept = -5
    D. $m = 3$, y-intercept = 5

Answer: C   Section 9.4

16. Find the slope and the y-intercept of the line having the given equation: $x - 3y = 12$
    A. $m = -1/3$, y-intercept = -4
    B. $m = 1/3$, y-intercept = -4
    C. $m = -3$, y-intercept = 4
    D. $m = 3$, y-intercept = -4

Answer: B   Section 9.4

17. Find the slope and the y-intercept of the line having the given equation: $x - y + 7 = 0$
    A. $m = 1$, y-intercept = 7
    B. $m = 1$, y-intercept = -7
    C. $m = -1$, y-intercept = -7
    D. $m = -1$, y-intercept = 7

Answer: A   Section 9.4

18. Find the slope and the y-intercept of the line having the given equation: $x = 5$
    A. $m = 0$, no y-intercept
    B. $m = 0$, y-intercept = 5
    C. $m =$ undefined, no y-intercept
    D. $m =$ undefined, y-intercept = 5

Answer: C   Section 9.4

19. Write the equation of the line through the point $(0, 4)$ having a slope of -3
    A. $y = -3x + 4$
    B. $y = -3x + 4$
    C. $y = 4x - 3$
    D. $y = 4x + 3$

Answer: A   Section 9.5

20. Write the equation of the line through the point $(2, -1)$ having a slope of 3
    A. $y = 3x + 7$
    B. $y = -3x + 7$
    C. $y = 3x - 7$
    D. $y = -3x - 7$

Answer: C   Section 9.5

21. Write the equation of the line through the point $(4, -1)$ having a slope of 0
    A. $y = 4$
    B. $y = 0$
    C. $x = 4$
    D. $y = -1$

Answer: D   Section 9.5

22. Write the equation of the line containing the points:
    (-2, 1), (3, -9)
    A. y = -2x + 1
    B. y = -2x - 3
    C. y = -1/2 x + 1
    D. y = -1/2 x + 5

Answer: B   Section 9.5

23. Determine whether the following pairs of lines :
    $y = \frac{1}{2}x - 3$ and $y = \frac{1}{2}x + \frac{1}{3}$ are:
    A. parallel
    B. perpendicular
    C. neither
    D. none of the above

Answer: A   Section 9.5

24. Write the equation of the line which passes through (-3, 5)
    and does not cross the x-axis.
    A. x = -3
    B. x = 5
    C. y = -3
    D. y = 5

Answer: D   Section 9.5

25. Ed Boofint earns a salary of $10,000 per year and an extra
    $3000 for each house sold. Write an equation relating the
    number of houses sold to Ed's salary.
    A. y = 10,000x + 3000
    B. y = 10,000x - 3000
    C. y = 3000x + 10,000
    D. y = -3000x + 10,000

Answer: C   Section 9.6

26. Ed Boofint earns a salary of $10,000 per year and an extra
    $3000 for each house sold. How much will Ed earn if he
    sells 4 houses in one year?
    A. $22,000
    B. $12,000
    C. $43,000
    D. $14,000

Answer: A   Section 9.6

27. Colleen earns $300 if she doesn't enter any bike races. If
    she enters ten bike races, she earns $1500. Write an
    equation expressing the linear relationship between the
    number of races Colleen enters and her earnings.
    A. y = 300x + 1500
    B. y = 1500x + 300
    C. y = 120x + 300
    D. y = 120x + 1500

Answer: C   Section 9.6

28. Graph: y ≤ x - 3

A.

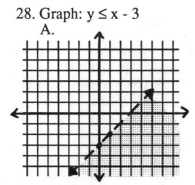

B.

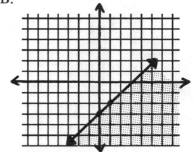

C.

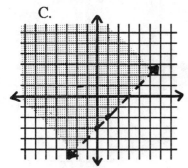

D.

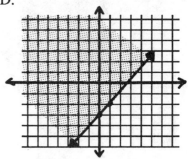

Answer: B   Section 9.7

29. Graph: y + 2x < 3

A.

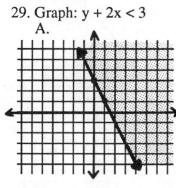

B.

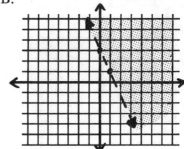

C.

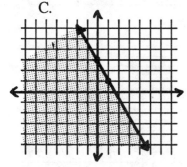

D.

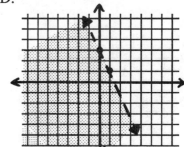

Answer: D   Section 9.7

30. Graph: x < 3

A.

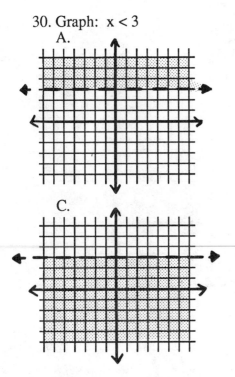

B.

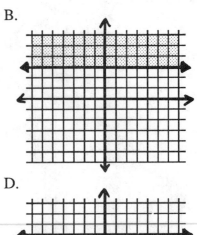

C.

D.

Answer: C   Section 9.7

31. Graph: x ≤ 4

A.

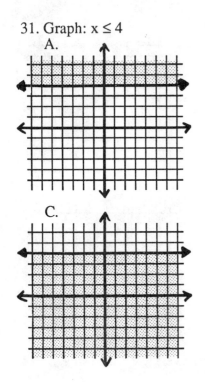

B.

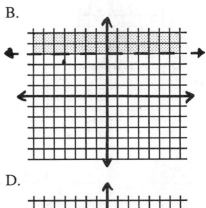

C.

D.

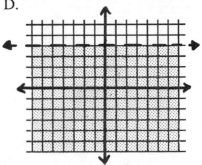

Answer: C   Section 9.7

164

Chapter 9 Problems

Section 9.1

32. Draw a set of axes, label them properly, and locate the points:
    (3, 7), (-2, -4), (4, -5), (-2, 0), (-2, -3).

33. Draw a set of axes, label them properly, and locate the points:
    (4, -1.2), (-3, $6\frac{1}{2}$), ($\frac{3}{2}$, -$\frac{3}{2}$), (0, 0), (-2.1, -2.1)

34. Find the ordered pairs representing the points on the following graph:

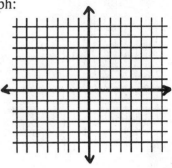

Section 9.2

35. Graph: x + y = 2

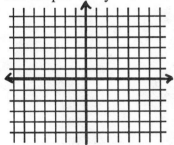

36. Graph: y - 2x = 4

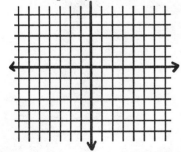

37. Graph: $6x - 3y = 9$

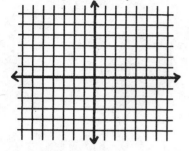

38. Graph: $x = 0$

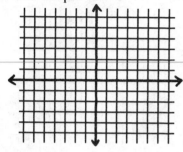

39. Graph: $y = -1$

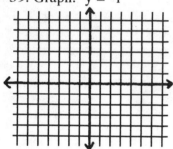

40. Graph: $y - x = 0$

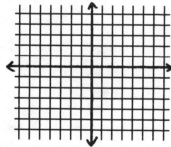

166

Section 9.3

41. Find the slope of the line through the points: (3, -4), (5, 7)

42. Find the slope of the line through the points: (0, 7), (-5, 6)

43. Find the slope of the line through the points: (5, 5), (-5, -5)

44. Find the slope of the line through the points: (0, -3), (0, 4)

Section 9.4

45. Find the slope and y-intercept of the line having the equation: $3x - 4y = 8$

46. Find the slope and y-intercept of the line having the equation: $y = -2x$

47. Find the slope and y-intercept of the line having the equation: $y = -2$

48. Find the slope and y-intercept of the line having the equation: $y = -\frac{1}{2}x + 4$

49. Find the slope and y-intercept of the line having the equation: $\frac{2}{3}x - \frac{1}{2}y + \frac{4}{3} = 0$

50. Graph: $y = 3x - 4$

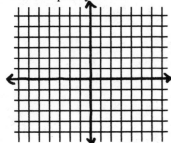

51. Graph: $y = 5x$

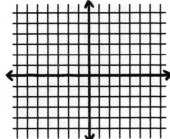

52. Graph: $y = -\dfrac{2}{3}x + 1$

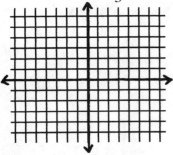

53. Graph: $x = -\dfrac{1}{2}$

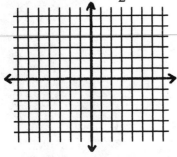

54. Graph: $x = 0$

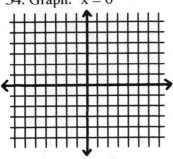

55. Graph: $y = -3$

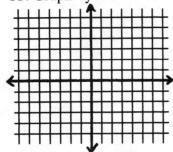

56. Graph: $3x - 4y = 4$

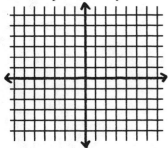

57. Graph: $y - 2x = 0$

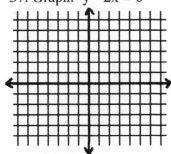

Section 9.5

58. Write the equation of the line through the point $(0, 0)$, having a slope of 2/3.

59. Write the equation of the line through the point $(-3, 4)$, having a slope of- 1/6.

60. Write the equation of the line through the point $(-1, -3)$, having a slope of -2.

61. Write the equation of the line through the point $(-2, 3)$, having an undefined slope.

62. Write the equation of the line containing the points: $(3, 6)$ $(2, 5)$

63. Write the equation of the line containing the points: $(-1, -3)$ $(4, 7)$

64. Write the equation of the line containing the points: $(4, 3)$ $(4, -2)$

65. Write the equation of the line containing the points: $(-3, 5)$ $(7, 5)$

66. Determine whether the following pairs of lines are parallel, perpendicular, or neither:
    $y - 3x = 7$ and $-2y + 6x = 2$.

67. Determine whether the following pairs of lines are parallel, perpendicular, or neither:
    $2x - y = 4$ and $x + 2y = -1$.

68. Write the equation of the line which passes through $(2, -3)$ and does not cross the y-axis.

169

69. Write the equation of any line perpendicular to y = -3x + 7.

70. Write the equation of any line that is parallel to 3x - 4y + 8 = 0.

Section 9.6

71. Nora, a bicycle mechanic earns $10 per day plus $1.50 for each bicycle she fixes. Write an equation that relates the number of bicycles Nora fixes to her daily income. How much would Nora earn if she fixed five bicycles?

72. The Rent-A-Klunk car rental agency charges $25 per day plus 3¢ per mile to rent a Red Bangup car. Write an equation that relates the total rental charge for one day to the number of miles driven. How much would a person pay if they drove 300 miles in one day?

73. If one cup of flour is used in Aunt Molly's chocolate cake recipe, 1 teaspoon of baking soda is needed. If six cups of flour are used, 4 teaspoons of baking soda are needed. The relationship between cups of flour and teaspoons of baking soda needed is linear. Write an equation which relates cups of flour to teaspoons of baking soda. How many teaspoons would be needed for 2 cups flour?

Section 9.7

74. Graph: y > 2x + 1

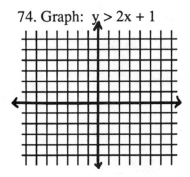

75. Graph: y ≥ -3x + 4

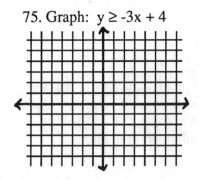

76. Graph: 2y - 3x > 8

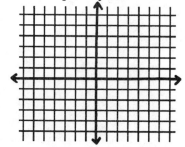

77. Graph: 5x - 10y ≥ 20

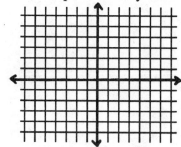

78. Graph: 5x - y ≤ 3

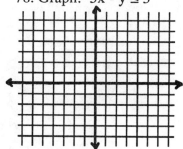

79. Graph: x ≥ -2

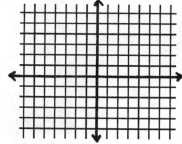

80. Graph: y > -1

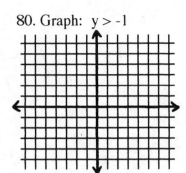

Answers

Chapter 9 Problems

32.

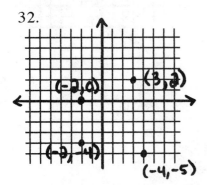

(-2, 0)   • (3, 3)

(-3, -4)

(-4, -5)

33.

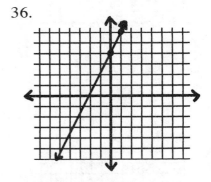

$(-3, 6\frac{1}{2})$

• $(\frac{3}{2}, \frac{1}{2})$

(0, 0)

(4, -1.2)

34. A: (-3, 2) B: (0, -1) C: (4, 1) D: (-2, -2)

35.

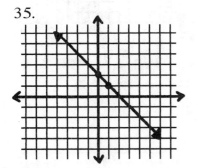

36.

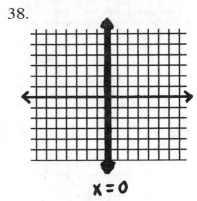

37.

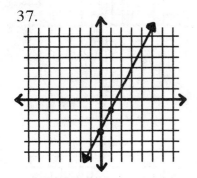

38.

x = 0

39.

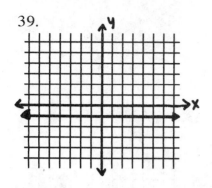

40.

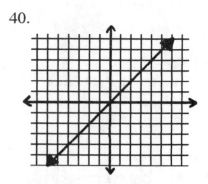

41. 11/2   42. 1/5   43. 1   44. undefined   45. m = 3/4, y-int. = -2   46. m = -2, y-int. = 0

47. m = 0, y-int. = -2   48. m = -1/2, y-int. = 4   49. m = 4/3, y-int. = 8/3

50.

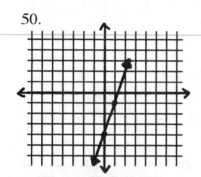

51.

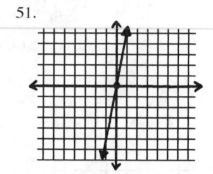

52.

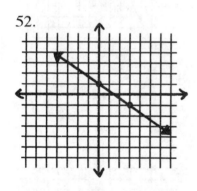

53.

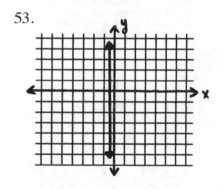

54.

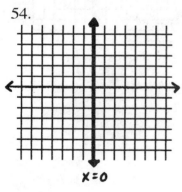

X = 0

55.

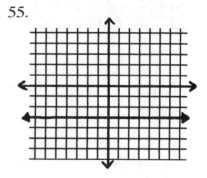

56.

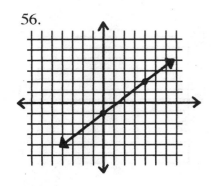

57.

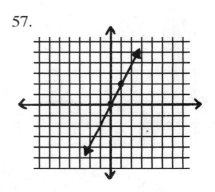

58. y = (2/3)x   59. y = (-1/6)x + 7/2   60. y = -2x - 5   61. x = -2   62. y = x + 3

63. y = 2x - 1   64. x = 4   65. y = 5   66. parallel   67. perpendicular   68. x = 2

69. y = (1/3)x + b, where b is any real number.   70. y = (3/4)x + b, where b is any real number.

71. y = 1.5x + 10, $17.50   72. y = 0.03x + 25, $34   73. y = (3/5)x + (2/5), 8/5 cups of flour.

74.

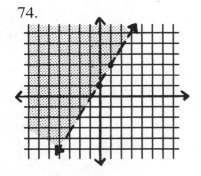

75.

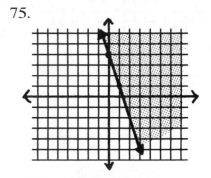

76.

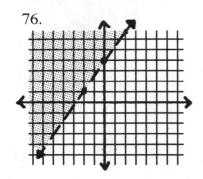

77.

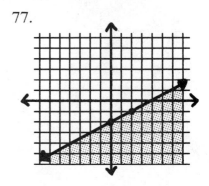

78.

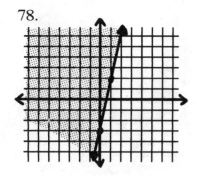

79.

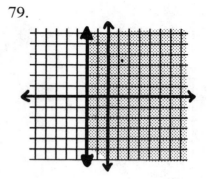

80.

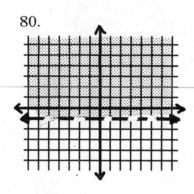

Chapter 10 Test Bank

Multiple Choice

1. The following pair of equations are: $y = 3x - 4$
$y = -3x + 5$

   A. intersecting
   B. parallel
   C. coincident

Answer: A   Section 10.1

2. The following pair of equations are: $3x - y = 4$
$-6x + 2y = -8$

   A. intersecting
   B. parallel
   C. coincident

Answer: C   Section 10.1

3. The following pair of equations are: $y = \frac{2}{3}x - 4$
$y = -\frac{3}{2}x + 1$

   A. intersecting
   B. parallel
   C. coincident

Answer: A   Section 10.1

4. The following pair of equations are: $2x - y = 3$
$-6x + 3y = -3$

   A. intersecting
   B. parallel
   C. coincident

Answer: B   Section 10.1

5. Solve by graphing: $y - 3x = -4$
   $6x - 2y = 1$

A. $(\frac{1}{2}, -2\frac{1}{2})$

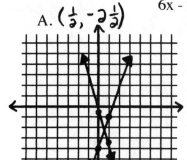

B. parallel, no solution

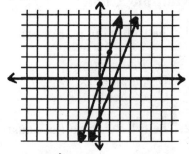

C. $(2, 2)$

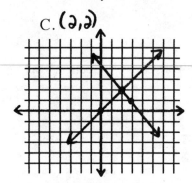

D. $(-2, 3)$

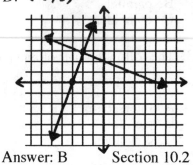

Answer: B   Section 10.2

6. Solve by graphing: $y - 2x = 2$
   $y + 2x = -6$

A. $(2, -2)$

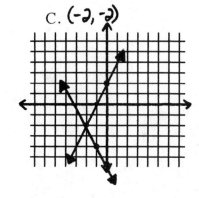

B. $(-2, 1)$

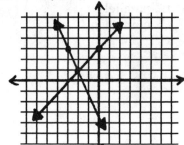

C. $(-2, -2)$

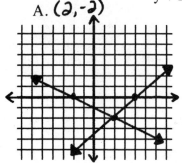

D. $(1, -2)$

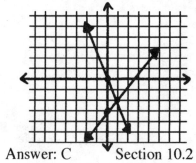

Answer: C   Section 10.2

178

7. Solve by graphing: $y - x = 0$
$3y + x = 12$

A. $(-1, -1)$

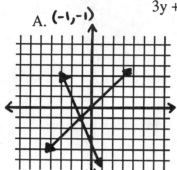

B. $(3, -4)$

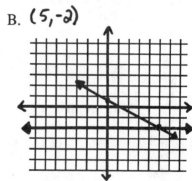

C. $(1, 1)$

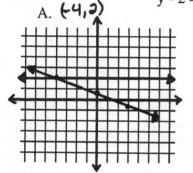

D. $(3, 3)$

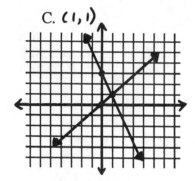

Answer: D   Section 10.2

8. Solve by graphing: $x + 3y = 2$
$y - 2 = 0$

A. $(-4, 2)$

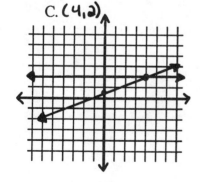

B. $(5, -2)$

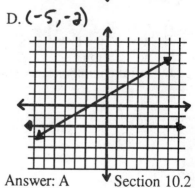

C. $(4, 2)$

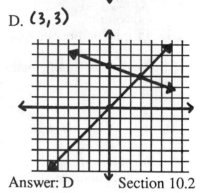

D. $(-5, -2)$

Answer: A   Section 10.2

179

9. Solve the system of equations using the addition method:
x + y = 9
x - y = 5

A. x = 7, y = 2
B. x = 14, y = -5
C. no solution
D. infinite number of solutions

Answer: A   Section 10.3

10. Solve the system of equations using the addition method:
2x - 3y = 1
3x + 2y = 8

A. x = 13, y = -9
B. x = 2, y =1
C. no solution
D. infinite number of solutions

Answer: B   Section 10.3

11. Solve the system of equations using the addition method:
3x - y = 7
-6x + 2y = -14

A. x = 13, y = -9
B. x = -9, y =13
C. no solution
D. infinite number of solutions

Answer: D   Section 10.3

12. Solve the system of equations using the addition method:
-7x + 14y = 3
x - 2y = -3

A. x = 13, y = -9
B. x = -9, y =13
C. no solution
D. infinite number of solutions

Answer: C   Section 10.3

13. Solve the system of equations using the addition method:
2x + 3y = 1
-4x + y = 5

A. x = 7/8, y = 3/2
B. x = -1, y =1
C. no solution
D. infinite number of solutions

Answer: B   Section 10.3

14. Solve the system of equations using the substitution method:
$x = 3y + 1$
$2y + 2x = -6$

A. $x = -14/8$, $y = -7/8$
B. $x = -2$, $y = -1$
C. no solution
D. infinite number of solutions

Answer: B   Section 10.4

15. Solve the system of equations using the substitution method:
$x - y = 51$
$y = x + 3$

A. $x = -14$, $y = -11$
B. $x = 24$, $y = 27$
C. no solution
D. infinite number of solutions

Answer: C   Section 10.4

16. Solve the system of equations using the substitution method:
$3x - y = 5$
$2x + 3y = -4$

A. $x = 1$, $y = -2$
B. $x = 1$, $y = 2$
C. no solution
D. infinite number of solutions

Answer: A   Section 10.4

17. Solve the system of equations using the substitution method:
$x + y = 10$
$x = 10 - y$

A. $x = -10$, $y = 20$
B. $x = 10$, $y = 0$
C. no solution
D. infinite number of solutions

Answer: D   Section 10.4

18. The sum of two numbers is 29. Their difference is -1.
Find the numbers.
A. 14, 15
B. 10, 19
C. 19, 18
D. 13, 16

Answer: A   Section 10.5

19. The perimeter of a rectangle is 32 cm. If one side is three times larger than the other, find the dimensions.
   A. 8cm, 24cm
   B. 2cm, 6cm
   C. 4cm, 12cm
   D. 6cm, 10cm

Answer: C   Section 10.5

20. Twelve quarters and dimes are worth $1.95. How many of each coin are there?
   A. 4 quarters and 8 dimes
   B. 7 quarters and 5 dimes
   C. 8 quarters and 4 dimes
   D. 5 quarters and 7 dimes

Answer: D   Section 10.5

21. The Hooting Twirlers charge $5 for children, and $10 for adults to attend their show. Sixty-five people attended, and receipts totalled $565. How many adults and children attended?
   A. 25 adults, 40 children
   B. 48 adults, 17 children
   C. 12 adults, 53 children
   D. 56 adults, 9 children

Answer: B   Section 10.5

22. Belinda is ten times as old as her grand-daughter, Maggie. In 3 years, Belinda will be three more than 7 times Maggie's age. Find out how old Belinda and Maggie are.
   A. Belinda 60, Maggie 6
   B. Belinda 70, Maggie 7
   C. Belinda 80, Maggie 8
   D. Belinda 90, Maggie 9

Answer: B   Section 10.5

Chapter 10 Problems

Section 10.1

23. Determine if the following pairs of equations are intersecting, parallel, or coincident:
$x - 2y + 4 = 0$
$3x + y = 2$

24. Determine if the following pairs of equations are intersecting, parallel, or coincident:
$4x - y = 2$
$y = 4x - 3$

25. Determine if the following pairs of equations are intersecting, parallel, or coincident:
$\frac{1}{3}x - \frac{1}{2}y = 5$
$\frac{2}{3}x - y = -10$

26. Determine if the following pairs of equations are intersecting, parallel, or coincident:
$3x + y = -2$
$2y = -4 - 6x$

Section 10.2

27. Solve the following systems by graphing: $4y - x = 0$
$y - x + 3 = 0$

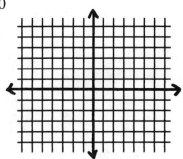

28. Solve the following systems by graphing: $-2y + 4x = -6$
$4x + 6 = 2y$

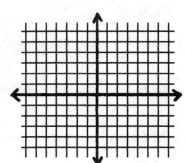

29. Solve the following systems by graphing: $y + 3x = 3$
$y - x = -1$

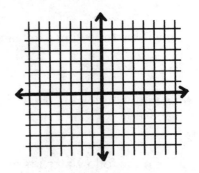

30. Solve the following systems by graphing: $y - x = 0$
$2y + x = 6$

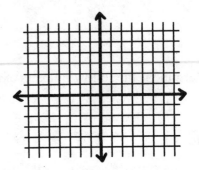

31. Solve the following systems by graphing: $x - 3y = 1$
$x + y = -3$

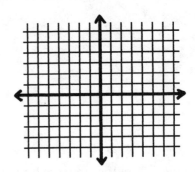

Section 10.3

32. Solve the following systems using the addition method: $x - 2y = 5$
$x + y = -1$

33. Solve the following systems using the addition method: $4x + 6y = -10$
$-2x - 3y = 4$

34. Solve the following systems using the addition method: $3x + y = 9$
$-2x - y = -3$

35. Solve the following systems using the addition method: $4x - y = 13$
$2x + 3y = -4$

36. Solve the following systems using the addition method: $5x + 2y = -4$
$$3x + 5y = 2$$

37. Solve the following systems using the addition method: $x + 5y = -3$
$$-3x - 15y = 9$$

Section 10.4

38. Solve the following systems using the substitution method: $2x + 3y = -3$
$$-x + y = 4$$

39. Solve the following systems using the substitution method: $4x - 8y = -12$
$$-2x + 4y = 6$$

40. Solve the following systems using the substitution method: $y = x - 1$
$$3x + y = 9$$

41. Solve the following systems using the substitution method: $2x + y = -1$
$$y = 4 - 2x$$

42. Solve the following systems using the substitution method: $2x - y = 4$
$$4x - 2y = 8$$

43. Solve the following systems using the substitution method: $5x + y = 7$
$$3x - y = 49$$

44. Solve the following systems using the substitution method: $2x + 2y = 0$
$$4x - 3y = 14$$

Section 10.5

45. The sum of two numbers is 66. If one number is nine less than twice the other number, find the numbers.

46. The length of a rectangle is three more than twice the width. If the perimeter is 36 yards, find the dimensions of the rectangle.

47. There is a collection of 28 one dollar and twenty dollar bills. How many of each do you have if their total value is $161?

48. Stay-green grass seed costs $3.50 per kg. Gro-slow grass seed costs $7 per kg. A 10 kg mixture of both seeds costs $56. How many kg of each type of seed is in the 10 kg bag?

49. The sum of two angles is 112°. The difference in the angles is 18°. Find the angles.

50. Danny's age is four times Carina's age. In six years, Danny will be four less than twice Carina's age. Find out how old Danny and Carina are.

Answers

Chapter 10 Problems

23. intersecting   24. parallel   25. parallel   26. coincident

27. (-4, -1)

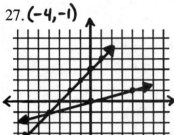

28. infinite solutions

29. (1, 0)

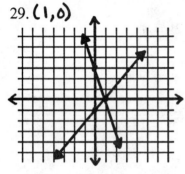

30. (4, 4)

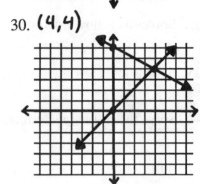

31. (-2, -1)

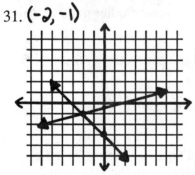

32. (1, -2)   33. no solution   34. (6, -9)   35. (5/2, -3)   36. (-8/5, 2)

37. infinite number of solutions   38. (-3, 1)   39. infinite number of solutions   40. (5/2, 3/2)

41. no solution   42. infinite number of solutions   43. (7, -28)   44. (2, -2)   45. 41, 25

46. 5 yards by 13 yards   47. 21 one dollar bills, 7 twenty dollar bills

48. 4 kg Stay-green, and 6 kg Gro-slow   49. 65°, 47°   50. Carina 1 year , Danny 4 years

Chapter 11 Test Bank

Multiple Choice

1. Evaluate: $\sqrt{25}$

   A. 5
   B. -5
   C. 5 and -5
   D. undefined

   Answer: A   Section 11.1

2. Evaluate: $\sqrt{-49}$

   A. 7
   B. -7
   C. 7 and -7
   D. undefined

   Answer: D   Section 11.1

3. Evaluate: $-\sqrt{64}$

   A. 8
   B. -8
   C. 8 and -8
   D. undefined

   Answer: B   Section 11.1

4. Simplify: $\sqrt{y^2}$

   A. y
   B. -y
   C. | y |
   D. undefined

   Answer: C   Section 11.1

5. Simplify: $\sqrt{(-3)^2}$

   A. 3
   B. -3
   C. 3 and -3
   D. undefined

   Answer: A   Section 11.1

6. Simplify: $\sqrt{x^2 - 9}$

   A. x - 3
   B. x + 3
   C. can't simplify
   D. undefined

   Answer: C   Section 11.1

7. The number 1.3636 . . . is:
   A. Real
   B. Rational and Real
   C. Irrational and Real
   D. Not Real

Answer: B   Section 11.2

8. The number 7/5 is:
   A. Real
   B. Rational and Real
   C. Irrational and Real
   D. Not Real

Answer: B   Section 11.2

9. The number π is:
   A. Real
   B. Rational and Real
   C. Irrational and Real
   D. Not Real

Answer: C   Section 11.2

10. The number $\sqrt{-4}$ is:

   A. Real
   B. Rational and Real
   C. Irrational and Real
   D. Not Real

Answer: D   Section 11.2

11. The number $-\sqrt{16}$ is:

   A. Real
   B. Rational and Real
   C. Irrational and Real
   D. Not Real

Answer: B   Section 11.2

12. The number 4.3172 . . . is:
   A. Real
   B. Rational and Real
   C. Irrational and Real
   D. Not Real

Answer: C   Section 11.2

13. The number 10.5121221222 . . . is:
   A. Real
   B. Rational and Real
   C. Irrational and Real
   D. Not Real

Answer: C   Section 11.2

14. Simplify: $\sqrt{56}$

    A. $7\sqrt{8}$
    B. $14\sqrt{2}$
    C. $2\sqrt{14}$
    D. $4\sqrt{14}$

Answer: C   Section 11.3

15. Simplify: $\sqrt{45ab^4}$
    A. $3b^2\sqrt{5a}$
    B. $9b^4\sqrt{5a}$
    C. $3b^4\sqrt{5a}$
    D. $3b^2\sqrt{15a}$

Answer: A   Section 11.3

16. Simplify: $\sqrt{a^8}$
    A. a^8
    B. a^4
    C. a^2
    D. a

Answer: B   Section 11.3

17. Multiply and Simplify: $\sqrt{10} \cdot \sqrt{14}$
    A. $\sqrt{140}$
    B. $4\sqrt{35}$
    C. $2\sqrt{35}$
    D. $2\sqrt{70}$

Answer: C   Section 11.3

18. Multiply and Simplify: $\sqrt{4a^2b} \cdot \sqrt{3ab^3}$
    A. $\sqrt{12a^3b^4}$
    B. $2ab\sqrt{3b}$
    C. $\sqrt{12a^2b^3}$
    D. $2ab^2\sqrt{3a}$

Answer: D   Section 11.3

19. Combine where possible: $4\sqrt{3} - 5\sqrt{3}$
    A. $\sqrt{3}$
    B. $-\sqrt{3}$
    C. $-9\sqrt{3}$
    D. can't combine

Answer: B   Section 11.4

20. Combine where possible: $\sqrt{75} - 2\sqrt{5}$
    A. $5\sqrt{3}$
    B. $3\sqrt{3}$
    C. $\sqrt{3}$
    D. can't combine

Answer: D   Section 11.4

21. Combine where possible: $4\sqrt{20x} - 3\sqrt{45x}$
   - A. $2x\sqrt{5}$
   - B. $-\sqrt{5x}$
   - C. $-2\sqrt{15x}$
   - D. can't combine

Answer: B   Section 11.4

22. Divide and Simplify: $\dfrac{\sqrt{75}}{\sqrt{3}}$
   - A. 5
   - B. -5
   - C. 5 and -5
   - D. can't simplify

Answer: A   Section 11.5

23. Divide and Simplify: $\sqrt{\dfrac{25}{49}}$
   - A. 7/9
   - B. 7/5
   - C. 5/7
   - D. 5/9

Answer: C   Section 11.5

24. Divide and Simplify: $\dfrac{\sqrt{90a^4}}{\sqrt{10a^2}}$
   - A. $9a^2$
   - B. $3a^2$
   - C. $9a$
   - D. $3a$

Answer: D   Section 11.5

25. Rationalize the denominator and simplify: $\dfrac{\sqrt{4}}{\sqrt{3}}$
   - A. $\dfrac{\sqrt{12}}{3}$
   - B. $\dfrac{2\sqrt{3}}{3}$
   - C. $3\sqrt{2}$
   - D. $\sqrt{6}$

Answer: B   Section 11.5

26. Rationalize the denominator and simplify: $\sqrt{\dfrac{3}{7}}$
   - A. $\sqrt{3}$
   - B. $\dfrac{\sqrt{3}}{7}$
   - C. $\dfrac{\sqrt{21}}{7}$
   - D. $\sqrt{21}$

Answer: C   Section 11.5

27. Rationalize the denominator and simplify: $\dfrac{\sqrt{5}}{\sqrt{36y}}$

    A. $\sqrt{15y}$

    B. $\dfrac{\sqrt{5y}}{6y}$

    C. $\dfrac{\sqrt{30y}}{6y}$

    D. $\sqrt{180y}$

                                 Answer: B   Section 11.5

28. Multiply and simplify: $\sqrt{3}\,(4 - \sqrt{6}\,)$

    A. $\sqrt{12} - 3\sqrt{2}$
    B. $4\sqrt{3} - \sqrt{18}$
    C. $2\sqrt{3} - 3\sqrt{2}$
    D. $4\sqrt{3} - 3\sqrt{2}$

                                 Answer: D   Section 11.6

29. Multiply and simplify: $(\sqrt{5} - 3)(\sqrt{5} + 4\,)$

    A. $-7 - \sqrt{5}$
    B. $-7 + \sqrt{5}$
    C. -7
    D. $\sqrt{25} - 7$

                                 Answer: B   Section 11.6

30. Multiply and simplify: $(\sqrt{7} + 3)^2$

    A. $16 + 6\sqrt{7}$
    B. $58 + 9\sqrt{7}$
    C. 58
    D. $\sqrt{49} + 58$

                                 Answer: A   Section 11.6

31. Rationalize the denominators and simplify: $\dfrac{3}{\sqrt{3} - 2}$

A. $-3\sqrt{3} - 6$

 B. $\dfrac{\sqrt{9} - 6}{7}$

 C. $\dfrac{\sqrt{9} - 6}{9}$

D. $\dfrac{3\sqrt{3} - 2}{7}$

                                 Answer: A   Section 11.6

32. Rationalize the denominators and simplify: $\dfrac{x - 3\sqrt{2}}{x + 3\sqrt{2}}$

    A. $-6\sqrt{2}$

    B. $\dfrac{x^2 - 6\sqrt{2} + 18}{x^2 - 18}$

    C. $\dfrac{x^2 - 3\sqrt{2}}{x^2 - 18}$

    D. $\dfrac{x^2 - 3\sqrt{2}}{x^2 - 36}$

Answer: B   Section 11.6

33. Solve and check: $\sqrt{x} = 5$

    A. $x = 5$
    B. $x = 25$
    C. $x = -25$
    D. no solution

Answer: B   Section 11.7

34. Solve and check: $\sqrt{x + 1} = -2$

    A. $x = -3$
    B. $x = 3$
    C. $x = -2$
    D. no solution

Answer: D   Section 11.7

35. Solve and check: $4 - \sqrt{x + 2} = 3$

    A. $x = -1$
    B. $x = 1$
    C. $x = 2$
    D. no solution

Answer: A   Section 11.7

36. Solve and check: $\sqrt{2x + 3} = \sqrt{x - 5}$

    A. $x = -8$
    B. $x = 8$
    C. $x = -2$
    D. no solution

Answer: D   Section 11.7

37. In a right triangle, if a and b represent legs and c represents the hypotenuse, find the length of the missing side when:
a = 12, b = 16
    A. 20
    B. 18
    C. 16
    D. 14

Answer: A   Section 11.8

38. In a right triangle, if a and b represent legs and c represents the hypotenuse, find the length of the missing side when:
a = 5, c = 13
A. 10
B. 12
C. 16
D. 14

Answer: B   Section 11.8

39. Determine whether the given triangle is a right triangle if:
a = 15, b = 10, c = 25
A. yes
B. no

Answer: B   Section 11.8

40. Determine whether the given triangle is a right triangle if:
a = 1, b = 2, c = $\sqrt{5}$
A. yes
B. no

Answer: A   Section 11.8

41. Find the measurment of the diagonal of a rectangle with length of 10m and width of 5m.

A. $\sqrt{15}$ m
B. $\sqrt{120}$ m
C. $5\sqrt{5}$ m
D. $3\sqrt{5}$ m

Answer: C   Section 11.8

Problems

Section 11.1

42. Evaluate: $\sqrt{4900}$

43. Evaluate: $\sqrt{100}$

44. Evaluate: $\sqrt{-4}$

45. Evaluate: $-\sqrt{25}$

46. Evaluate: $\sqrt{0}$

47. Simplify: $-\sqrt{16x^2}$

48. Simplify: $\sqrt{(-a)^2}$

49. Simplify: $\sqrt{x^2 - 9}$

50. Simplify: $\sqrt{x^2 - 6x + 9}$

Section 11.2

51. Is the number $14.6777\ldots$ rational, irrational?

52. Is the number 3π rational, irrational?

53. Is the number 5.3165 rational, irrational?

54. Is the number $4.3443444\ldots$ rational, irrational?

Section 11.3

55. Simplify: $\sqrt{300}$

56. Simplify: $\sqrt{x^2y^3}$

57. Multiply and simplify: $\sqrt{2x} \cdot \sqrt{18x^3}$

58. Multiply and simplify: $\sqrt{22x} \cdot \sqrt{x^3y^4} \cdot \sqrt{11x^2y}$

194

59. Multiply and simplify: $\sqrt{5x} \cdot \sqrt{6y} \cdot \sqrt{10x^2y}$

Section 11.4

60. Combine where possible: $2\sqrt{a} - 3\sqrt{b} + 4\sqrt{a}$

61. Combine where possible: $4\sqrt{18} + 3\sqrt{50}$

62. Combine where possible: $3\sqrt{12} - \sqrt{75} + \sqrt{25}$

Section 11.5

63. Divide and simplify: $\dfrac{\sqrt{200}}{\sqrt{50}}$

64. Divide and simplify: $\dfrac{\sqrt{35}}{\sqrt{5}}$

65. Divide and simplify: $\dfrac{\sqrt{14x^2y^3}}{\sqrt{6x^5y}}$

66. Divide and simplify: $\sqrt{\dfrac{40x^3y}{8xy^4}}$

67. Rationalize the denominator and simplify: $\dfrac{3\sqrt{6}}{\sqrt{2}}$

68. Rationalize the denominator and simplify: $\dfrac{4\sqrt{3}}{\sqrt{x}}$

69. Rationalize the denominator and simplify: $\sqrt{\dfrac{2}{25a}}$

Section 11.6

70. Multiply and simplify: $3\sqrt{x}\,(\sqrt{x} - \sqrt{3}\,)$

71. Multiply and simplify: $4\sqrt{5}\,(3\sqrt{2} + 7\sqrt{10}\,)$

72. Multiply and simplify: $(3\sqrt{6} - 1)(2\sqrt{6} + 2)$

73. Multiply and simplify: $(\sqrt{2} - \sqrt{5})(\sqrt{2} + \sqrt{5}\,)$

74. Multiply and simplify: $(\sqrt{2} - 2\sqrt{5})^2$

75. Rationalize the denominator and simplify: $\dfrac{-2}{\sqrt{5} + 1}$

76. Rationalize the denominator and simplify: $\dfrac{\sqrt{5} + 2}{\sqrt{5} - 3}$

77. Rationalize the denominator and simplify: $\dfrac{4 - \sqrt{y}}{2 + \sqrt{y}}$

Section 11.7

78. Solve and check: $\sqrt{3a} = 2$

79. Solve and check: $\sqrt{x - 2} = 4$

80. Solve and check: $\sqrt{3x - 1} = 1$

81. Solve and check: $10 + \sqrt{1 - x} = 7$

82. Solve and check: $\sqrt{3x - 2} = \sqrt{x + 4}$

Section 11.8

83. In a right triangle if a and b represent legs, and c is the hypotenuse, find the length of the missing side for: $a = 2, b = 2$

84. In a right triangle if a and b represent legs, and c is the hypotenuse, find the length of the missing side for: $b = 4, c = 5$

85. In a right triangle if a and b represent legs, and c is the hypotenuse, find the length of the missing side for: $a = 3\sqrt{2}, b = \sqrt{7}$

86. In a right triangle if a and b represent legs, and c is the hypotenuse, find the length of the missing side for: $a = 3, c = 7$

87. Determine whether or not the given triangle is a right triangle: $a = 4, b = 5, c = 20$

88. Determine whether or not the given triangle is a right triangle: $a = 6, b = 8, c = 10$

89. Find the length of a square which has a diagonal of 10 cm.

90. How long must a ladder be to reach 8 ft up the side of the house if the base of the ladder is 6 feet from the base of the house.

Answers

Chapter 11 Problems

42. 70   43. 10   44. undefined   45. -5   46. 0   47. $-4|x|$ 48. $|a|$ 49. can't simplify

50. $|x - 3|$ 51. rational   52. irrational   53. irrational   54. irrational

55. $10\sqrt{3}$ 56. $xy\sqrt{y}$ 57. $6x^2$ 58. $11x^3y^2\sqrt{2y}$

59. $10xy\sqrt{3x}$ 60. $6\sqrt{a} - 3\sqrt{b}$ 61. $27\sqrt{2}$ 62. $\sqrt{3} + 5$ 63. 2   64. $\sqrt{7}$ 65. $\dfrac{y}{x}\sqrt{\dfrac{7}{3x}}$

66. $\dfrac{x}{y}\sqrt{\dfrac{5}{y}}$ 67. $3\sqrt{3}$ 68. $\dfrac{4\sqrt{3x}}{x}$ 69. $\dfrac{\sqrt{2a}}{5a}$ 70. $3x - 3\sqrt{3x}$ 71. $12\sqrt{10} + 140\sqrt{2}$

72. $34 + 4\sqrt{6}$ 73. -3   74. $22 - 4\sqrt{10}$ 75. $\dfrac{-2\sqrt{5} + 2}{4}$ 76. $\dfrac{11 + 5\sqrt{5}}{-4}$ 77. $\dfrac{8 - 6\sqrt{y} + y}{4 - y}$

78. $\dfrac{4}{3}$ 79. 18   80. $\dfrac{2}{3}$ 81. no solution   82. 3   83. $2\sqrt{2}$

84. 3   85. 5   86. $2\sqrt{10}$ 87. no   88. yes   89. $\sqrt{5}$ cm   90. 10ft

Chapter 12 Test Bank

Multiple Choice

1. Write the equation in standard form: $x = 5x^2 - 7$
   A. $5x^2 - 7 - x = 0$
   B. $5x^2 - x - 7 = 0$
   C. $5x^2 + x - 7 = 0$
   D. $-5x^2 + x + 7 = 0$

   Answer: B   Section 12.1

2. Write the equation in standard form: $12 + 6x = 3x^2 + x$
   A. $3x^2 - 5x + 12 = 0$
   B. $-3x^2 + 5x + 12 = 0$
   C. $12 + -5x + 3x^2 = 0$
   D. $3x^2 - 5x - 12 = 0$

   Answer: D   Section 12.1

3. Write the equation in standard form: $\frac{2}{3}x - \frac{1}{2}x^2 = \frac{5}{6}$
   A. $3x^2 - 4x + 5 = 0$
   B. $4x^2 - 3x + 5 = 0$
   C. $-3x^2 + 4x - 5 = 0$
   D. $-4x^2 + 3x - 5 = 0$

   Answer: A   Section 12.1

4. Solve and check: $x^2 - 25 = 0$
   A. 5
   B. -5
   C. 5 and -5
   D. no solution

   Answer: C   Section 12.2

5. Solve and check: $x^2 + 3x - 4 = 0$
   A. -4, 1
   B. 4, -1
   C. -4
   D. no solution

   Answer: A   Section 12.2

6. Solve and check: $y^2 - 6y = 0$
   A. 6
   B. -6
   C. 6, 0
   D. no solution

   Answer: C   Section 12.2

7. Solve and check: $4x^2 + x = 6 + 2x^2$
   A. 3, -2
   B. 3/2, -2
   C. 2/3, -2
   D. no solution

   Answer: B   Section 12.2

8. Solve and check: $5x^2 - 20 = 0$
   A. 2, -2
   B. -2
   C. 2
   D. no solution

9. Solve and check: $25x^2 = 15$
   A. $\dfrac{3}{5}$
   B. $\dfrac{3\sqrt{5}}{5}$, $\dfrac{-3\sqrt{5}}{5}$
   C. $\dfrac{3\sqrt{5}}{5}$
   D. no solution

10. Solve and check: $(x - 4)^2 = 9$
    A. 7
    B. 1
    C. 7, 1
    D. no solution

11. Complete the square: $x^2 - 6x + \underline{\hspace{1cm}} =$
    A. $(x - 9)^2$
    B. $(x - 3)^2$
    C. $(x + 9)^2$
    D. $(x + 3)^2$

12. Complete the square: $x^2 + 5x + \underline{\hspace{1cm}} =$
    A. $(x - \dfrac{5}{2})^2$
    B. $(x - \dfrac{25}{4})^2$
    C. $(x + \dfrac{5}{2})^2$
    D. $(x - \dfrac{25}{4})^2$

13. Solve by completing the square: $y^2 - 6y - 7 = 0$
    A. 7
    B. -1
    C. 7, -1
    D. -7, 1

14. Solve by completing the square: $x^2 - 5x + 1 = 0$

   A. $\dfrac{5 + \sqrt{21}}{2}, \dfrac{5 - \sqrt{21}}{2}$

   B. $\dfrac{5 + \sqrt{29}}{2}, \dfrac{5 - \sqrt{29}}{2}$

   C. $\dfrac{-5 + \sqrt{21}}{2}, \dfrac{-5 - \sqrt{21}}{2}$

   D. $\dfrac{-5 + \sqrt{29}}{2}, \dfrac{-5 - \sqrt{29}}{2}$

Answer: A   Section 12.4

15. Solve by completing the square: $m^2 + 3m - 2 = 0$

   A. $\dfrac{3 + \sqrt{17}}{2}, \dfrac{3 - \sqrt{17}}{2}$

   B. 2, 1

   C. $\dfrac{-3 + \sqrt{17}}{2}, \dfrac{-3 - \sqrt{17}}{2}$

   D. -1, -2

Answer: C   Section 12.4

16. Solve by completing the square: $3x^2 - 7x + 1 = 0$

   A. $\dfrac{7 + \sqrt{61}}{2}, \dfrac{7 - \sqrt{61}}{2}$

   B. $\dfrac{7 + \sqrt{37}}{6}, \dfrac{7 - \sqrt{37}}{6}$

   C. $\dfrac{-7 + \sqrt{37}}{6}, \dfrac{-7 - \sqrt{37}}{6}$

   D. $\dfrac{-7 + \sqrt{61}}{6}, \dfrac{-7 - \sqrt{61}}{6}$

Answer: B   Section 12.4

17. Solve using the quadratic formula: $x^2 + x - 3 = 0$

   A. $\dfrac{1 + \sqrt{13}}{2}, \dfrac{1 - \sqrt{13}}{2}$

   B. $\dfrac{1 + \sqrt{11}}{2}, \dfrac{1 - \sqrt{11}}{2}$

   C. $\dfrac{-1 + \sqrt{13}}{2}, \dfrac{-1 - \sqrt{13}}{2}$

   D. $\dfrac{-1 + \sqrt{11}}{2}, \dfrac{-1 - \sqrt{11}}{2}$

Answer: C   Section 12.5

18. Solve using the quadratic formula: $7b^2 + 4b - 3$

   A. 1, - 3/7

   B. -1, -3/7

   C. 1, 3/7

   D. -1, 3/7

Answer: D   Section 12.5

19. Solve using the quadratic formula: $(x - 2)^2 = 2(5 + x)$

    A. $3 + \sqrt{3}, \; 3 - \sqrt{3}$
    B. $-3 + \sqrt{3}, \; -3 - \sqrt{3}$
    C. $-3 + \sqrt{15}, \; -3 - \sqrt{15}$
    D. $3 + \sqrt{15}, \; 3 - \sqrt{15}$

Answer: D   Section 12.5

20. Solve and check: $x + 3 = \dfrac{4}{x}$

    A. 4
    B. 4, -1
    C. -4, 1
    D. no solution

Answer: C   Section 12.6

21. Solve and check: $\dfrac{9}{x + 3} = \dfrac{x^2}{x + 3}$

    A. 3
    B. -3
    C. 3, -3
    D. no solution

Answer: A   Section 12.6

22. Solve and check: $\dfrac{-28}{x^2 - 1} + 1 = \dfrac{5}{x + 1}$

    A. -3
    B. 8
    C. 8, -3
    D. no solution

Answer: C   Section 12.6

23. Solve and check: $\dfrac{2}{x^2 - 9} = \dfrac{1}{x + 3} + \dfrac{3}{x - 3}$

    A. -1
    B. 3
    C. -3
    D. no solution

Answer: A   Section 12.6

24. Solve and check: $\sqrt{x^2 - 11} = 6$

    A. $\sqrt{47}$
    B. $-\sqrt{47}$
    C. $\sqrt{47}, \; -\sqrt{47}$
    D. no solution

Answer: C   Section 12.7

25. Solve and check: $x = \sqrt{3x + 4}$

    A. -1
    B. 4
    C. 4, -1
    D. no solution

Answer: B   Section 12.7

26. Solve and check: $2\sqrt{x} = x + 2$

    A. 4
    B. -2
    C. 2
    D. no solution

Answer: D   Section 12.7

27. The sum of the squares of two positive consecutive odd integers is 130. Find the integers.
    A. -7, -9
    B. 7, 5
    C. 7, -9
    D. 7, 9

Answer: D   Section 12.8

28. The hypotenuse of a right triangle is 8 cm greater than one of the legs. If the other leg is 12 cm, find the lengths of the other sides.
    A. 13 cm, 5 cm
    B. 15 cm, 5 cm
    C. 8 cm, 13 cm
    D. 12 cm, 8 cm

Answer: A   Section 12.8

29. A picture is 10 inches by 8 inches. The matte around the picture is of uniform width. The area of the matte and the picture is equal to 224 in^2. Find the width of the matte.
    A. 12 in
    B. 4 in
    C. 3 in
    D. 2 in

Answer: C   Section 12.8

30. Sketch the graph of: $y = x^2 - 4$

A.

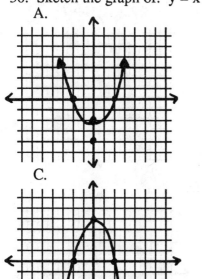

B.

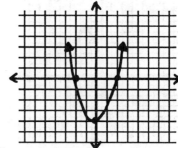

C.

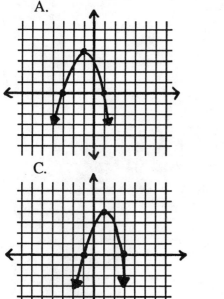

D.

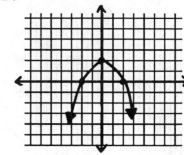

Answer: B   Section 12.9

31. Sketch the graph of: $y = -x^2 + 2x + 3$

A.

B.

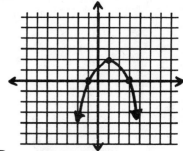

C.

D.

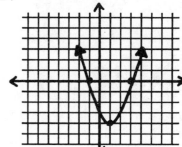

Answer: C   Section 12.9

33. Sketch the graph of: $y = -2x^2 + 6x$

A.

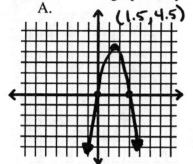

(1.5, 4.5)

B.

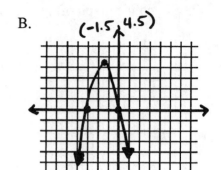

(-1.5, 4.5)

C.

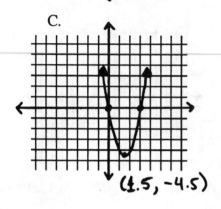

(1.5, -4.5)

D.

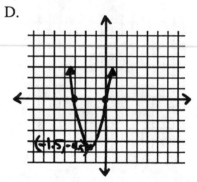

(-1.5, -4.5)

Answer: A   Section 12.9

Chapter 12 Problems

Section 12.1

33. Write the equation $3 - 2x^2 + 7x = 0$ in standard form, and identify a, b, and c.

34. Write the equation $-2(x - 3) = x^2 - 7x + 4$ in standard form, and identify a, b, and c.

35. Write the equation $25 = 4x^2$ in standard form, and identify a, b, and c.

36. Write the equation $\frac{1}{4}x^2 + \frac{1}{6} = \frac{1}{2}x + \frac{1}{4}$ in standard form, and identify a, b, and c.

Section 12.2

37. Solve and check: $x^2 = 100$

38. Solve and check: $7y^2 = 49y$

39. Solve and check: $3x^2 - x - 2 = 0$

40. Solve and check: $\frac{2}{3}x^2 = 4 - \frac{5x}{3}$

Section 12.3

41. Solve and check: $3y^2 = 27$

42. Solve and check: $4x^2 - 5 = 0$

43. Solve and check: $(x + 2)^2 = 16$

44. Solve and check: $(x + 1)^2 - 3 = 0$

45. $5x^2 - 12 = 0$

Section 12.4

46. Complete the square: $x^2 + 12x + \underline{\quad} = (x + \underline{\quad})^2$

47. Complete the square: $x^2 + x + \underline{\quad} = (x + \underline{\quad})^2$

48. Complete the square: $x^2 - 3x + \underline{\quad} = (x - \underline{\quad})^2$

49. Complete the square: $x^2 + \frac{2}{3}x + \underline{\quad} = (x + \underline{\quad})^2$

50. Solve by completing the square: $w^2 + 8w - 3 = 0$

51. Solve by completing the square: $2x^2 - 12x + 3 = 0$

52. Solve by completing the square: $3y^2 - y - 2 = 0$

53. Solve by completing the square: $4x^2 - 6x - 3 = 0$

Section 12.5

54. Solve using the quadratic formula: $x^2 - 3x + 2 = 0$

55. Solve using the quadratic formula: $3y^2 - 2y - 1 = 0$

56. Solve using the quadratic formula: $3b^2 + 3b - 3 = 0$

57. Solve using the quadratic formula: $4y^2 - 3y = y^2 + 2y - 1$

58. Solve using the quadratic formula: $x^2 - 2(x + 1) = 5x$

59. Solve using the quadratic formula: $(x - 2)^2 = 2(5 + x)$

60. Solve using the quadratic formula: $(x + 3)(2x - 1) = 5x - 3$

Section 12.6

61. Solve and check: $x - \dfrac{4}{x} = 3$

62. Solve and check: $\dfrac{1}{x} - \dfrac{2}{3} = \dfrac{x}{3}$

63. Solve and check: $\dfrac{2}{x} - \dfrac{1}{4} = \dfrac{2}{x}$

64. Solve and check: $1 - \dfrac{3}{x + 4} = \dfrac{-14}{x^2 - 16}$

65. Solve and check: $\dfrac{-49}{x - 7} = \dfrac{-x^2}{x - 7}$

Section 12.7

66. Solve and check: $\sqrt{3x^2 - 26x} = 3$

67. Solve and check: $\sqrt{3x + 1} = 2x$

68. Solve and check: $x + 1 = \sqrt{-3x - 5}$

69. Solve and check: $1 + y = \sqrt{1 + y}$

Section 12.8

70. The product of two positive consecutive even integers is 168. Find the integers.

71. The length of a rectangle is two more than four times the width. If the area is 20 m^2, find the length of the sides.

72. A group of bicyclists travel 20 miles out to a restaurant, with a 5 mph wind blowing against them. Then they ride 20 miles with the wind at their back. If the trip took a total of 3 hours, how fast would they ride with no wind?

Section 12.9

73. Sketch the graph of: $y = x^2 + 4x - 12$

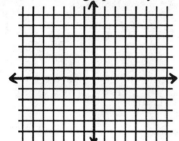

74. Sketch the graph of: $y = x^2 + 2$

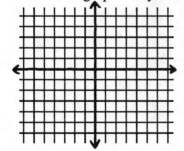

75. Sketch the graph of: $y = 3x^2 - 1$

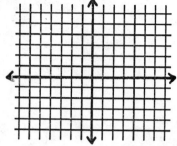

76. Sketch the graph of: $y = -3x^2 + 8x - 5$

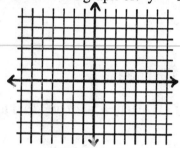

77. Sketch the graph of: $y = x^2 - 2x - 15$

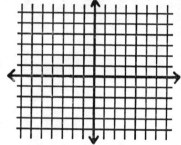

Answers

Chapter 12 Problems

33. $2x^2 - 7x - 3 = 0$, $a = 2$, $b = -7$, $c = -3$ 34. $x^2 - 5x - 2 = 0$, $a = 1$, $b = -5$, $c = -2$

35. $4x^2 + 0x - 25 = 0$, $a = 4$, $b = 0$, $c = -25$ 36. $3x^2 - 6x - 1 = 0$, $a = 3$, $b = -6$, $c = -1$

37. $10, -10$ 38. $0, 7$ 39. $-2/3, 1$ 40. $3/2, -4$ 41. $3, -3$

42. $\dfrac{\sqrt{5}}{2}, -\dfrac{\sqrt{5}}{2}$ 43. $2, -6$ 44. $-1 + \sqrt{3}, -1 - \sqrt{3}$ 45. $\dfrac{2\sqrt{15}}{5}, -\dfrac{2\sqrt{15}}{5}$

46. $36, 6$ 47. $\dfrac{1}{4}, \dfrac{1}{2}$ 48. $\dfrac{9}{4}, \dfrac{3}{2}$ 49. $\dfrac{1}{9}, \dfrac{1}{3}$ 50. $-4 + \sqrt{19}, -4 - \sqrt{19}$ 51. $\dfrac{6 + \sqrt{30}}{2}, \dfrac{6 - \sqrt{30}}{2}$

52. $-\dfrac{2}{3}, 1$ 53. $\dfrac{3 + \sqrt{21}}{4}, \dfrac{3 - \sqrt{21}}{4}$ 54. $2, 1$ 55. $1, -\dfrac{1}{3}$ 56. $\dfrac{-1 + \sqrt{5}}{2}, \dfrac{-1 - \sqrt{5}}{2}$

57. $\dfrac{5 + \sqrt{13}}{6}, \dfrac{5 - \sqrt{13}}{6}$ 58. $\dfrac{7 + \sqrt{57}}{2}, \dfrac{7 - \sqrt{57}}{2}$ 59. $3 + \sqrt{15}, 3 - \sqrt{15}$ 60. 0

61. $4, -1$ 62. $1, -3$ 63. no solution   64. $5, -2$ 65. -7 66. $-1/3, 9$ 67. 1

68. no solution   69. $0, -1$ 70. $12, 14$ 71. 2 m by 10 m   72. 15 mph

73.
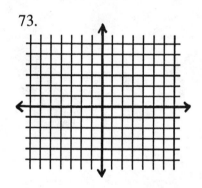

74.
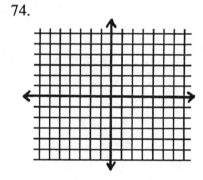

75.
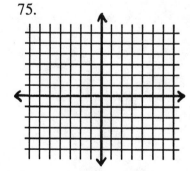

76.
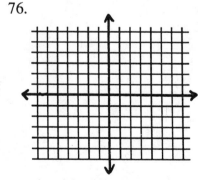

77.

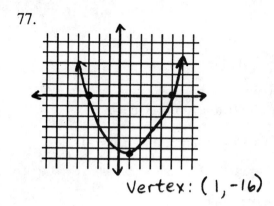

Vertex: (1, -16)